Th

The Art of Struggle

MICHEL HOUELLEBECQ

Translated by

Delphine Grass
and
Timothy Mathews

HERLA

Published by
HERLA PUBLISHING, an imprint of

ALMA BOOKS LTD
London House
243-253 Lower Mortlake Road
Richmond
Surrey TW9 2LL
United Kingdom
www.oneworldclassics.com

First published in French as *Le Sens du Combat* by Flammarion in 1996
French text © Flammarion, 1996
This English translation first published by Alma Books Limited in 2010
English translation and Introduction
© Delphine Grass and Timothy Mathews, 2010

This book is supported by the French Ministry of Foreign Affairs, as part of the Burgess programme run by the Cultural Department of the French Embassy in London. (www.frenchbooknews.com).

Printed in Great Britain by TJ International, Padstow, Cornwall

ISBN: 978-1-84688-106-0

All rights reserved. No part of this publication may be reproduced, stored in or introduced into a retrieval system, or transmitted, in any form or by any means (electronic, mechanical, photocopying, recording or otherwise), without the prior written permission of the publisher. This book is sold subject to the condition that it shall not be resold, lent, hired out or otherwise circulated without the express prior consent of the publisher.

Contents

Translators' Foreword	v
The Art of Struggle	1
I	3
II	35
III	99
IV	147

Translators' Foreword

I

Michel Houellebecq is well known and in fact notorious as a novelist in the English-speaking world. In spite of his three books of poetry, few readers are aware of him as a poet. In reality, it is as a poet that Houellebecq started his career and began to make his name in Parisian literary circles. After publishing his poetry manifesto *Rester Vivant* in 1991 (*Staying Alive*), Houellebecq went on to publish his first collection of poems, *La Poursuite du bonheur*, in 1992 (*The Pursuit of Happiness*). *The Art of Struggle*, originally entitled *Le Sens du combat*, was published in 1996 after his first successes as a novelist. It went on to be the first collection of poems to win the Prix de Flore. In 1999, by now established as a novelist – thanks to *Extension du domaine de la lutte* (*Whatever*), in 1994, and *Les Particules élémentaires* (*Atomised*) in 1998 – Michel Houellebecq published *Renaissance*, *Re-Birth*, his third and last book of poetry to date.

At the time of the release of Houellebecq's first books of poems and novels, an intense web of debate had developed around sexuality and emotion based on the ideals of freedom inherited from the 1960s. Mixed with the rising impetus of free-market globalization, the texture of the language used in this debate was almost featureless. Its aim was to universalise human affect into a set of communicable and easily manageable psychological truths. It set out to influence the most intimate aspect of our lives. Self-help books and commercial psychoanalysis became the first port of call when things did not feel right, and there was a sense that perhaps a more gentle and politically correct form of consumerism could cure the ills of consumerism itself. In the midst of such a culture came Houellebecq, a depressed, nonchalant figure whose very way of smoking cigarettes – holding them between his middle and ring finger – seemed to signal his dissent from the world.

An animosity began to grow against Houellebecq in the media, and one of the reasons was that Houellebecq had an opposing vision of contemporary modernity from the prevalent talk of "diversity" and "multiculturalism". As the title of his novel *Platform* (published originally as *Plateforme* in 2001) encapsulates, the content of all his novels suggests that the feel of the world is becoming more and more homogenous. The world has been standardized rather than enriched by the growing network of media communication. This idea of homogeneity translates for Houellebecq into the most intimate aspects of our sense of self. As he put it in an interview with the novelist and critic Philippe Sollers, his works convey the intuition that "today, we can no longer experience desire independently from advertising". Generally, as his eponymous character in *Platform* suggests, Michel Houellebecq has a strong "inkling that more and more, the whole world would come to resemble an airport".

Like Baudelaire, his greatest poetic influence, Houellebecq is the aesthetic ambassador of his own modernity. His attitude to life has trickled into a singular way of writing. Like his own demeanour, Houellebecq's poetry exacerbates rather than reconciles the discrepancies between the projection of happiness constructed by consumer society and his personal and contemplative experience of it. During his appearances on French television at the time of the release in the Nineties of his first two novels, Houellebecq gave a fascinating depiction of someone who had not so much overcome as mastered the ills of his own depression, to the extent that depression had itself become an art. As a poet Houellebecq noticeably shapes his emotional nonconformity into a critique of the world which has made him, and he makes his social inadequacies into his choice of weapon. In French, "sens" can mean either "way" or "sense", and "combat" can mean "struggle" or "fight". *Le Sens du combat* conveys Houellebecq's will to carve out and sculpt a place for collective feelings of discontent within a consumer-driven, universalizing appropriation of affect.

As many of his critics have observed, Houellebecq unashamedly projects his own dejection into his works. The same could be said of *The Art of Struggle*. But in return for these intense, dismal bouts of subjectivism, Houellebecq manages to seize, internalize and depict human beings' emotional relationship with the fleeting nature of the global free market. But what is there to be mourned, one might ask, in everything that we gain from the constant renewal of objects and possibilities? Houellebecq's answer is developed from a different premise. What we fail to mourn in our sense of constant growth and expansion is for him the kernel of our discontent. In insisting on his own sense of loss in a world of abundance, Houellebecq shows that no authentic form of renewal or regeneration can occur without formulating and accepting the value of what is left behind. The invariable celebration characteristic of consumerism changes our capacity to experience loss into a form of melancholia arising from our failure to mourn. At their best, the poems of *The Art of Struggle* are able to express these unprocessed feelings with simple and moving irony:

> I'll go home with my lungs
> The tiles will be freezing.
> As a child I loved sweets
> And now nothing matters.

There is a sense in *The Art of Struggle* that the most direct way of incarnating these feelings of unmourned loss is in lyrical form. By giving a recognizable form to loss, Houellebecq's lyricism opens the invisible and often disowned side of our consumerism to criticism and change. Houellebecq's poems are thus not a window onto his own internal doom. They shape his darkest intuitions into light, illuminating and clarifying in the process some of the most dismaying aspects of our contemporary culture. For that reason, and in spite of the palpable sadness of some of the poems, Houellebecq's lyricism is both aesthetically and intellectually stimulating for the light it throws on our collective experience of modernity as a paradoxical form of loss through gain.

One idea which Houellebecq grapples with in *The Art of Struggle* is that we do not only live in a free-market economy but a free-market society, where human beings themselves have been integrated within a system of exchange. His evocation of modern architecture is particularly telling in relation to this vision. In his essay 'Approches du désarroi' ('An Approach to Dismay'), published in *Interventions* in 1998, Houellebecq describes the modern city, with its see-through architecture and its open-plan office spaces, as a set of structures operating with the same intent as supermarket shelves. This mental picture is translated, so to speak, into the following line in the first poem of *The Art of Struggle*: "Nous sommes prisonniers de notre transparence" ("We're prisoners of our own clear selves"). It is thus not surprising to see in the poems that the GAN Tower has replaced the Eiffel Tower as the authentic emblem of modern Paris. The GAN Tower is in La Défense, an area of Paris which Houellebecq knows well for having worked there as a computer programmer before making a living from his writing.

At first glance, Houellebecq's poetic endeavours might seem to have stopped in 1999. But in fact poetry has remained an essential part of his project as a novelist. Poems are often inserted in the novels and at times, as is the case in *La Possibilité d'une île* (*The Possibility of an Island*), published in 2005, they can play a major role in the plot itself. This dialogue between prose and poetry is significant in the writing of *The Art of Struggle*, and the poems echo some of the themes and characters in his novels. Prose poems also hold a significant place in Houellebecq's poetry: the subjectivity of his novelistic prose is soaked in the sensibility of his poems. There is no explicit narrative or plot in *The Art of Struggle*, yet one can identify a path, a progression in the way that the poems enrich and support each other's craft. As the poem shows called 'So Long' in French, 'A Long Farewell to the Sound of Poets', *The Art of Struggle* develops a wider conversation with literary tradition as a form of collective memory. Houellebecq's aim is not to inform our lives with the grandeur of past poetic exploits in a way that might leave us feeling impoverished, or more frustrated still with our day to day lives. In their generous approach to form, the poems incorporate tradition within the living scope of the reader's everyday life in such a way that it can be experienced as a tangible collective legacy.

II

Translating poetry is often thought of as especially difficult or even pointless: poetry seems to rely so much on tone, and rhythm, and sometimes rhyme rather than the combination purely of meanings. To translate poetry is to be immersed in the power of words and their forms, and poetry shows the power of words to reveal everything that separates us as well as everything we share. In translating *The Art of Struggle*, our main concern was to capture its tone, the attitude of the poet towards his subject, the way the poem makes meaning in the way it sounds.

But tone itself is produced in various forms and structures which themselves do not translate transparently from French into English. This is true of prose as well as verse, although especially evident in verse. Many readers will know that French verse is organised differently from English. In the French language the metre of a line of poetry or a whole poem is created on the basis of the number of syllables in the line, while English verse is organised according to the number of stressed and unstressed syllables in the line. Stress is produced in the poetry of both languages, and rhythm created in the interplay of the stressed and the unstressed. But rhythm is not produced in the same way, nor heard in the same way.

One way to respond is to adopt a meter in English appropriate to the metre of any particular poem in French. Perhaps the iambic pentameter produces the same canonical effect, the same effect of tradition and history, as the alexandrine in French, for example. But we did not want to impose one way of hearing any particular metre in either language. Metre is at the heart of the verse poems of Michel Houellebecq's book. We wanted to communicate the way the book uses metre to give substance to the sound of the voice, to the way sensation is communicated, and thinking, as well as a sense of imprisonment or blindness.

But still, the voice will not sound the same in different languages, nor will the memory of people speaking have the same resonances for any one of us. We have adopted meters which to us seemed flexible enough to convey the sound of reading each one of Houellebecq's verse poems – the sound of reading aloud, or silently; or the effects of hearing the poem reverberate. Sometimes a four-stressed line seemed right in response the twelve-syllable French alexandrine, established in French neo-Classicism, brutalized in French Romanticism. But sometimes a three-stress line seemed right, for Houllebecq like others hears the possibilities of the alexandrine in response to the rhythms of the voice, whether a spoken voice or an inner one. Sometimes his poems in the eight-syllable meter need a four-stress line to come to life in English, it seemed to us; but sometimes three – the eight-syllable line in French has a history stretching back through Symbolism and Romanticism to the Renaissance and beyond, and can be made to sound differently in response to different experiences and associations. For the duration of our journey in English through each one of Houellebecq's poems in French we stayed with the meter we chose, or rather which imposed itself on us; and tried to stay alert to variety and surprise as well. That has been our way of recreating the effects of Houellebecq's attraction to the various French metres in this book; and his ability to stretch them, remould them and renew them.

But what about rhyme? Rhyme and metre often work in an inseparable counterpoint, and that is true of Houellebecq's poetry as well. But it is not true of all verse poetry. And the networks of rhyme and meaning are not, cannot be the same in different languages. Rhyme can create hidden association in one language where in another, a rhyme at the equivalent point might create a kind of deafness to the association stumbled upon originally. In translating poetry the relation of rhyme to meaning asks questions of the translator which have no answer, and also of the reader. Sound or meaning?

But sound is in the service of meaning, the sound reverberates because of the meanings discovered. This is language, not music: that is the approach taken here to translating *Le Sens du combat* (*The Art of Struggle*), the ways high and low of the struggle which Houellebecq charts. It is a struggle to give voice to depersonalization, and to personhood; to the futility of private emotion and the futility of life without it; to the competition between economic and affective humanity. There is a journey in Houellebecq's book, and although there is no departure or arrival, there is rhythm; a rhythm of vacuity – disheartening, or witty – and weight: an oppressive weight, which is also the weight of meaning, of experience, and the ways of affirming your own living and dying in a body, and in a voice.

This is a journey in poetry, and in our translation of this journey meaning leads sound, even though the meaning is made in sound, in poetry. As much as metre, we have translated rhyme into the presence of rhyme; this has been our way of affirming Houellebecq's poetry and the poetic in general, of affirming a way of thinking which has broken its dependency on directives, whether spoken or beyond the telling. Or can that dependency ever be broken? Poetry invites alertness, an intimate and unresolved questioning, and the alertness we offer here to the effects of rhyme is a presence of sound patterns in the poems in English. We hope they will speak to the explicit rhymes of Houllebecq's poems, and to the invitations of poetry to hear, hear differently, to hear our own familiarity with life and meaning, differently.

The rhymes and rhythms of poetry are as much to do with the memory of them as with hearing them again now. But memory can be a tired one as much as an illuminating and energizing one. And love-hate relations with the traditions of verse and its assumptions are prompted differently in different languages. Here the conversation is limited to English and French ways of writing poetry, but the differences are still as palpable as ever. How to translate not just a rhythm but a way of hearing it?

Translation is made in the moment when the uniqueness of a word sounds differently to different people. In prose poetry as much as in verse, the rhythms of spoken language, of internal monologue, of the memories of emotion and response, are not the same in any two languages. Idioms are not heard alike by two individuals, even if we are each aware of those differences and use them to communicate. It is not a question of being faithful or treacherous to the original; for how could we agree on what that faithfulness would be? This is not only an effect of translation, but part and parcel of the language we use generally; the language we use to communicate thoughts which are no longer there and which as a reader you will not have witnessed in the making. We communicate, agree or disagree on the basis of the relations, distances and proximities which we sense in relation to our own experience, and which we sense we might share with others; or we might resent others for not responding as we do to this sense of relation. Conversation arises from the way we hear differently, and such is the way of translation too.

We have tried to translate not just words but effects; not just sentences but structures. "How would you say that in English?" The question is both a necessary and a treacherous one. If I say something as I think you would, or I would, or if I said it in a way I hope you will understand, I am appropriating something as much as translating it and disseminating it, I am making it mine as much as giving something to you in an untampered state. "How would you say that?" – the question engages in an immediate way both with what is lost and gained in translation. Without asking the question we would not be translating but glossing, in a way, giving a literal account not only of meanings but of the way sentences and verses are put together in French; trying to preserve familiar expressions and impressions which will only be foreign in another language. Without asking the question "How would you say that?" we would not be translating but obfuscating, giving in to the illusion that how things sound in French or any language can be transported into any other without sounding simply unusual, or worse still quaint, a kind of tourist, arm's-length appreciation of French. But our purpose is to translate Houellebecq's injunction to the reader to engage.

How is an allusion heard – and how is it heard in different languages? It may not be heard at all. What is familiar to one reader may be unknown to another. The success of an allusion is even more tenuous in translation and in the attempt to carry it over from one language to another. One translator may in any case hear different things from another. In addition to Baudelaire, Houellebecq's poetry in verse and prose waves to other poets in French, both in content and form, and they range from Villon, to Rimbaud, to Verlaine and to Ponge – or so it has appeared to us. Even if they are heard, allusions to French poets will not carry the same resonance in English as they do in French itself: think of Eliot's appropriation of poets in French and other languages. Allusion is another way for a poet to engage with the experience of readers, to invite readers to re-engage with what is familiar to them and with their own intimate memories. We have translated allusion into the presence of allusion, an invitation to readers to hear their own living responses. Echoes in English have emerged in the course of our translators' journey and we have allowed them to remain at various points, and hopefully to live. In that way we have tried to bear witness to Houellebecq's plea to his readers to engage with their own subjectivity.

In *The Art of Struggle* Michel Houellebecq is concerned with the loss of meaning and a return of the lyrical; with the loss of emotion and its return; with the loss of a sense of personhood and the mourning of the person. But the book is also a critique of the person and a critique of its mourning. When meaning is lost or being lost, the only thing left to hold on to is the forms of meaning, its now empty shells, empty of meaning, but not emotion. What once was meaningful is meaningful still in the gestures we retain, reminding us not so much of what it is we have lost but that we have lost something. What have we lost, then? A sense of self, its importance and its depth; and mourning is not enough to give it back its voice.

For Houellebecq, emotion seems to have been quantified in every way imaginable from desire on the one hand to delivery on the other. There is nothing left of us but what appears, or can be made to appear in habitual and consumerist responses so pervasive they are barely noticed. But *The Art of Struggle* is a struggle towards some sort of resistance, or an extended meditation on the possibility of resistance itself. The vocabulary of our attachments has become impoverished, it seems; how shall we even wish to respond to each other with desire rather than in slogans? The book offers a journey towards resistance and rebirth, to renewed despair as much as hope in its own increasing weight of emotion, and thought; in its own brutal as well as lyrical battles with complacency. Read as whole, as one might a novel, *The Art of Struggle* is a struggle in words with the power of words to limit and entice, to seduce and enthral. A systematic emptiness of experience, an implacably observed emptiness of meaning, grows into an investigation of social and emotional evolution: possible, or tragically unlikely?

We would like to thank Michel Houellebecq for suggesting that we translate this book, and for his support and his courtesy throughout. We would in all humility like to thank each other for what we have learnt in this process, as well as the following friends and colleagues for their generous encouragement and for reading parts of this work as it developed: Martin Crowley, Ruth Cruickshank, Jane Gilbert, Eivind Kahrs, John Kinsella, Rod Mengham; Chris Hamilton-Emery and everyone at *Salt Online*, where versions of our translations of "This man on the other platform...", "The swallows take their flight..." and "In the Service of Blood" were first published; and Alessandro Gallenzi at Alma Books for his consistent confidence in this project. Our thanks go also to our families who have lived this journey with us, and to friends in North and East London for their support and also shelter in times of small and grand adjustments.

– Delphine Grass, Timothy Mathews, July 2010

La Tour Gan, now called La Tour First, in La Défense, Paris

The Art of Struggle

I

Le jour monte et grandit, retombe sur la ville
Nous avons traversé la nuit sans délivrance
J'entends les autobus et la rumeur subtile
Des échanges sociaux. J'accède à la présence.

Aujourd'hui aura lieu. La surface invisible
Délimitant dans l'air nos êtres de souffrance
Se forme et se durcit à une vitesse terrible ;
Le corps, le corps pourtant, est une appartenance.

Nous avons traversé fatigues et désirs
Sans retrouver le goût des rêves de l'enfance
Il n'y a plus grand-chose au fond de nos sourires,
Nous sommes prisonniers de notre transparence.

Dawn rises, grows, settles on the city
We've come through the night and not been set free
I hear the buses and the quiet hum
Of social exchange. I'm overcome with presence.

Today will happen. Invisible surfaces
Separate our suffering selves in the air
Then form and harden at a terrible pace;
But the body, still our pact with the body.

We've come through strain and desire
Childhood and dreams still pass us by
Not much there in a lifetime of smiling
We're prisoners in our own clear selves.

Au long de ces journées où le corps nous domine
Où le monde est bien là, comme un bloc de ciment,
Ces journées sans plaisir, sans passion, sans tourment,
Dans l'inutilité pratiquement divines

Au milieu des herbages et des forêts de hêtres,
Au milieu des immeubles et des publicités
Nous vivons un moment d'absolue vérité :
Oui le monde est bien là, et tel qu'il paraît être.

Les êtres humains sont faits de parties séparables,
Leur corps coalescent n'est pas fait pour durer
Seuls dans leurs alvéoles soigneusement murés
Ils attendent l'envol, l'appel de l'impalpable.

Le gardien vient toujours au cœur du crépuscule ;
Son regard est pensif, il a toutes les clés,
Les cendres des captifs sont très vite envolées ;
Il faut quelques minutes pour laver la cellule.

Throughout those days when the body rules
When the world is like a block, so very there
Those joyless days, no passion, no torment
In their blankness so nearly divine,

In the midst of the clearings and forests
In the midst of the towers and the ads
Comes a moment of true understanding:
Oh yes, the world is there, just as it seems.

Human beings come in separate parts,
Congealing bodies are not built to last,
In their meticulous pods tidily sealed
They wait for take-off, the call of the untouched.

The guard always comes in the middle of sunset,
He looks likes he's thinking, and he's got all the keys,
The ashes of the inmates will quickly be gone,
It takes a few minutes to clean out the cell.

APRÈS-MIDI

Les gestes ébauchés se terminent en souffrance
Et au bout de cent pas on aimerait rentrer
Pour se vautrer dans son mal d'être et se coucher,
Car le corps de douleur fait peser sa présence.

Dehors il fait très chaud et le ciel est splendide,
La vie fait tournoyer le corps des jeunes gens
Que la nature appelle aux fêtes du printemps
Vous êtes seul, hanté par l'image du vide,

Et vous sentez peser votre chair solitaire
Et vous ne croyez plus à la vie sur la Terre
Votre cœur fatigué palpite avec effort

Pour repousser le sang dans vos membres trop lourds,
Vous avez oublié comment on fait l'amour,
La nuit tombe sur vous comme un arrêt de mort.

MID-AFTERNOON

Gestures half-form, then end up in suffering
After walking a bit you'd rather go home
To sprawl in depression and lie on your bed,
Your body of sorrow's heavy with presence.

Outside it's hot and the sky is magnificent,
Life puts the bodies of the young in a spin
And nature calls them to the rite of spring
You're alone, haunted by the image of nothing

And you feel the weight of flesh, and loneliness
And you don't believe in life on this earth
Your worn-out heart flutters and struggles

And makes your limbs go heavy with blood,
You've forgotten how people make love,
Night falls like a sentence of death.

CHÔMAGE

Je traverse la ville dont je n'attends plus rien
Au milieu d'êtres humains toujours renouvelés
Je le connais par cœur, ce métro aérien ;
Il s'écoule des jours sans que je puisse parler.

Oh ! ces après-midi, revenant du chômage
Repensant au loyer, méditation morose,
On a beau ne pas vivre, on prend quand même de l'âge
Et rien ne change à rien, ni l'été, ni les choses.

Au bout de quelques mois, on passe en fin de droits
Et l'automne revient, lent comme une gangrène ;
L'argent devient la seule idée, la seule loi,
On est vraiment tout seul. Et on traîne, et on traîne…

Les autres continuent leur danse existentielle,
Vous êtes protégé par un mur transparent ;
L'hiver est revenu. Leur vie semble réelle.
Peut-être, quelque part, l'avenir vous attend.

THE DOLE

I cross the city with nothing in mind
And the endless turnover of souls,
The overhead line, I know it by heart;
Days go by, I've nothing to say.

Oh, those afternoons coming back from the social
Thinking about rent and other morose doings,
Vegetate as much as you like, you're still getting older,
It doesn't change anything, neither summer, nor things.

A few months later you lose your benefits
Autumn comes back slowly like gangrene;
Money is the only thought, the only law,
You are really alone, and it lingers and insists.

The others go on in their existential ballet,
Behind the glass partitions you're sheltered away;
Winter is back. Their lives seem real.
Maybe, somewhere, your future is waiting.

Les moments immobiles que l'on vit presque en fraude
Et les petites morts, petits autodafés ;
C'était sur les deux heures et la ville était chaude,
Les bustiers fourmillaient aux terrasses des cafés

Et tout s'organisait pour la reproduction :
Comportements humains, jeux de dents, rires forcés
L'impossibilité permanente de l'action
Morceaux de vie qu'on rêve, bientôt désamorcés.

Les humains s'agitaient dans les murs de la ville :
Flots sur le boulevard, téléphones portatifs ;
Inquiétude sur la ligne, jeux de regards hostiles :
Tout fonctionne, tout tourne, et j'ai les nerfs à vif.

Sometimes we live in a fraudulent stillness
With little faints and little tortures
The cafés were swarming with cleavage,
Two o'clock and the city was hot

Everything was set for reproduction:
All teeth, behaviour and smiles
Everything made endlessly impossible
Fragments of a dream, soon unprimed.

Humans were busy in the walls of their city:
Crowds on the streets and mobile phones;
Anxiety all the way, hostility and looks:
Everything runs smooth, my nerves are raw.

Il marche dans la nuit, son regard plein de mort,
Et le froid se fait vif entre les carrefours
Cela fait plus d'un an qu'il n'a pas fait l'amour ;
Les êtres humains se croisent, on sent glisser leurs corps.

Il marche dans la ville avec un mot secret,
C'est vraiment très curieux de voir les autres vivre,
De regarder la vie comme on lit dans un livre
Et d'avoir oublié jusqu'au goût du regret.

Il compose le code, retrouve son studio
Et une main glacée se pose sur son cœur
Certainement quelqu'un a commis une erreur,
Il n'a plus très envie d'écouter la radio.

Il est seul, maintenant, et la nuit est immense
Il frôle les objets d'une main hésitante
Les objets sont bien là, mais sa raison s'absente
Il traverse la nuit à la recherche d'un sens.

He's walking at night, his eyes full of death,
The wind in the streets lashes his bones
Already a year without making love:
Humans brush past and slip round his body.

He's walking in the city with his own secret thought,
How interesting to see others live,
To look at life like reading a book
And even forget the taste of regret.

He punches the buttons and lets himself in
An icy breath settles on his soul
There must be a mistake, surely there must,
And the radio is getting him down.

Now he's alone and the night is immense
He skims over his things with a tentative hand
Yes they are there but his reason is not
He uses the night to look for a way.

AU SERVICE DU SANG

Je ne pars plus vraiment en voyage
Car je connais l'endroit
Et je connais mes droits,
Et j'ai connu la rage.

Au service de l'humanité,
Assis dans la cité,
Je connais bien ma chambre
Je sens la nuit descendre.

Les anges qui s'envolent
Dans la splendeur des cieux
Et qui retrouvent Dieu,
Les femmes qui rigolent.

Attaché à ma table,
Assis dans la cité,
La lente intensité
De la nuit implacable.

La nuit dans la cité,
La lente immensité,
La vision très cruelle
Détachée sur le ciel
D'une forme qui bouge
Qui palpite, qui est rouge.

Au service du sang,
Des dégoûts peu conscients,
Des fins d'amour cruelles
Des éclats du réel ;

IN THE SERVICE OF BLOOD

I no longer go on trips, really,
Because I know the place
And I know my rights,
And I've lived through rage.

In the service of humanity,
In the middle of the estate,
I know my bedroom well
And feel the night descend.

Angels take flight
In the glory of heaven
They will find God;
And the women have fun.

Tied to the table,
Sat in the estate,
The slow intensity
Of the relentless night.

At night in the estate
The slow immensity,
The cruel vision
Torn off from the sky
Of a shape that moves
Pulsating and red.

In the service of blood
The sleepy disgust,
The cruel ends of love
The blown-up bits of the real;

Tout cela pour quoi faire ?
L'idée d'une vision
La fin d'une chanson
Les hommes qui désespèrent

Qui attendent la rage
Et les corps éclatés
Qui s'accroupissent, blessés,
Dans l'espoir du carnage.

J'apporte l'aliment
De la haine finale,
Je fais frotter mes dents
Et je ressens le mal.

Je connais bien les ruses
De la chair écrasée
On me dit que j'abuse,
Je me sens justifié

Par l'humaine souffrance,
Par les espoirs déçus
Par l'écrasement dense
Des journées superflues.

Je ne suis pas serein,
Mais je suis dans ma chambre
Les anges me tiennent la main,
Je sens la nuit descendre.

And all that for what?
The idea of a vision
The end of a song
Men losing hope

Waiting for rage
For exploding bodies,
Squatting, wounded,
Hoping for carnage.

I bring the ingredient
Of the final hatred,
My teeth are grinding,
Evil seeps in.

I know the tricks
Of a crushed flesh
I overdo it, I'm told
But I feel exonerated

By human suffering,
By hopes dissatisfied
By the dense crushing
Of superfluous days.

I am not serene
But I am at home,
Angels are holding my hand
I can feel the night falling.

L'instant d'une renonciation, je m'abats sur la banquette. Cependant, les rouages du besoin se remettent à tourner. La soirée est fichue ; peut-être la semaine, peut-être la vie ; il n'empêche que je dois ressortir acheter une bouteille d'alcool.

De jeunes bourgeoises circulent entre les rayonnages du Monoprix, élégantes et sexuelles comme des oies. Il y a probablement des hommes, aussi ; je m'en fiche pas mal. On a beau ne plus imaginer de mots possibles entre soi et le reste de l'humanité, le vagin reste une ouverture.

Je remonte les étages, mon litre de rhum serré dans un sac plastique. Je me détruis, je le sens bien ; mes dents s'effritent. Pourquoi, aussi, mon regard fait-il fuir les femmes ? Le jugent-elles implorant, fanatique, coléreux ou pervers ? Je ne le sais pas, je ne le saurai probablement jamais ; mais ceci fait le malheur de ma vie.

I feel like giving up, and collapse on the back seat. But the wheels of need start turning again. The evening's ruined, maybe the week, maybe even the rest of my life, but I'll still need to go out again and get booze.

In Tesco a few yummy mummies are wondering in the aisles, refined and sexed up like peahens. There are probably a few men there too, but who cares? You can give up on small talk as much as you like, a vagina is still an opening.

I went up the stairs, clutching my litre of rum in its plastic bag. I'm killing myself, I can see that, my teeth have started to crumble. And when I look at women, why do they run away? Do they think I plead too much, or I'm desperate, have too much anger, or look like a perv? I've no idea. Probably never will. And that's the tragedy.

FIN DE SOIRÉE

En fin de soirée, la montée de l'écœurement est un phénomène inévitable. Il y a une espèce de planning de l'horreur. Enfin, je ne sais pas ; je pense.
L'expansion du vide intérieur. C'est cela. Un décollage de tout événement possible. Comme si vous étiez suspendu dans le vide, à équidistance de toute action réelle, par des forces magnétiques d'une puissance monstrueuse.

Ainsi suspendue, dans l'incapacité de toute prise concrète sur le monde, la nuit pourra vous sembler longue. Elle le sera, en effet.
Ce sera, pourtant, une nuit protégée ; mais vous n'apprécierez pas cette protection. Vous ne l'apprécierez que plus tard, une fois revenu dans la ville, une fois revenu dans le jour, une fois revenu dans le monde.
Vers neuf heures, le monde aura déjà atteint son plein niveau d'activité. Il tournera souplement, avec un ronflement léger. Il vous faudra y prendre part, vous lancer – un peu comme on saute sur le marchepied d'un train qui s'ébranle pour quitter la gare.
Vous n'y parviendrez pas. Une fois de plus, vous attendrez la nuit – qui pourtant, une fois de plus, vous apportera l'épuisement, l'incertitude et l'horreur. Et cela recommencera ainsi, tous les jours, jusqu'à la fin du monde.

END OF AN EVENING

At the end of the evening, nausea is the obvious prognosis. As though horror had its own schedule. Well I don't know, I'm thinking.
The black hole of the inner world is booming. That's it. The possibility of anything happening has come unstuck. As though you were suspended in the void by the forces of a monstrous magnetic power, permanently at arm's length from any real action.

Suspended without any foothold in the world, night might seem long to you. And in fact it will be.
It'll be a protected night, however, but you won't want that kind of protection. You'll only appreciate it later when you're back in the city, back in the day, back in the world.
At about nine, the world will already be going at full strength. It'll be turning over lithely, purring quietly. You'll have to take part, get involved – a bit like jumping onto the step of a moving train as it clatters out of the station.
You won't be able to. Once again you'll be waiting for the night, which once again will bring exhaustion, worry and horror.
And it'll be like that again, every day, until the end of the world.

Derrière mes dents et jusqu'au fond de ma gorge, mon palais est tapissé de ramifications brunes, rigidifiées et entremêlées comme des branches mortes ; mais à l'intérieur vit un nerf de douleur. Leurs indentations et leurs divisions sont si fertiles que les tiges forment un buisson touffu, comme une surface légèrement rugueuse au-dessus de la chair ; ces faibles tiges supportent à peine le poids du paquet de branches mortes qui les surmonte. La surface en dessous est sale, avec de gros grumeaux de crasse, des capsules et des bouteilles vides qui roulent et frappent les tiges, parcourant l'ensemble du massif d'un frémissement douloureux. Il y a même un os de seiche ; les ramifications ont poussé autour, se sont rigidifiées et durcies.

J'ai peur que quelqu'un vienne avec un peigne de métal et commence à le passer dans ce buisson. L'ensemble craquerait et s'arracherait de l'intérieur de ma bouche dans un jaillissement mou ; les racines de mes dents viendraient avec, tout s'arracherait et pendrait de ma bouche comme une masse de chair filamenteuse et saignante.

Behind my teeth and right down to the back of my throat my palate is papered with brown solid tendrils tangled up like dead branches. There's a raw nerve inside. The indentations of my teeth and the cracks between them have gone fertile, the stalks have formed a thick bush, like a rough patch of flesh. The wilting stalks can barely keep up the mass of dead branches weighing them down. The surface below is nasty, covered in lumps of filth. Empties and bottle tops roll around and collide with the stalks spreading a painful shudder over the whole mound. There's even a cuttlebone, the tendrils which have grown all around it have gone solid and hard.

I'm afraid someone's going to come along and comb this morass with a metal comb. The whole thing would break up and tear itself away from my mouth in a limp explosion; the roots of my teeth would follow and everything would tear itself away, hanging from my mouth in a mass of blood and stringy flesh.

Le lobe de mon oreille droite est gonflé de pus et de sang. Assis devant un écureuil en plastique rouge symbolisant l'action humanitaire en faveur des aveugles, je pense au pourrissement prochain de mon corps. Encore une souffrance que je connais mal et qui me reste à découvrir, pratiquement dans son intégralité.
Je pense également et symétriquement, quoique de manière plus imprécise, au pourrissement et au déclin de l'Europe.

Attaqué par la maladie, le corps ne croit plus à aucune possibilité d'apaisement. Mains féminines, devenues inutiles. Toujours désirées, cependant.

My right ear lobe is swollen with puss and blood. Sat in front the red plastic squirrel of Action for the Blind, I'm pondering on the imminent decay of my body. Another type of suffering I'm unfamiliar with and which remains to be discovered, pretty much completely.
I also ponder in exactly the same way, with equal interest though with less precision, on the rot and the decline of Europe.

Ravaged by disease, the body no longer hopes for peace. Women's hands – gone useless. Still desirable, however.

Bouche entrouverte, comme des carpes, nous laissons échapper des renvois de mort. Pour dissimuler l'odeur de mort qui sort de nos gueules, qui sort invinciblement de nos gueules, nous émettons des paroles.

Les pierres calcaires qui composent nos maisons sont des animaux morts. Des animaux écartelés, dépecés, desséchés ; des coquillages éviscérés. Des coquillages écrasés, triturés, malaxés par la violence interne de la terre ; par la terrifiante chaleur des entrailles de la terre. Des animaux conglomérés et morts.

Open-mouthed like carps we exhale the belches of the dead. To hide the smell of death coming out of our throats, coming undefeated from our throats, we use words.

We build our houses in limestone blocks of dead animals. The animals are quartered, disembowelled, bled dry; meat is torn off the shells. The shellfish are crushed, minced, kneaded by the inner violence of the earth; by the dreadful warmth in the guts of the earth. Mixed in a paste and dead.

UNE JOURNÉE AVEC ELLE

Elle me regarde, et son regard est plein de sang. Et sa viande excitante n'est qu'une enveloppe sur du sang. Je vois le sang qui coule de ses seins tranchés. Je vois le sang.

Elle est là. Le matin. Et le soir. Je m'éveille à huit heures du soir et je crois que c'est le matin. Non. C'est le soir. C'est toujours le soir.
C'est la nuit. Qui vient. Et qui n'est pas douce. La nuit avec ses marionnettes de sang ; les fils qui courent dans la chair translucide et jaune. Les marionnettes qui ressemblent à des femmes ; le sang qui coule, doucement, des marionnettes.

Matinée. Explosion. Bleu partout. Toujours du bleu ; splendide. Le jour qui recommence ; qui insiste. Quand viendra la douceur ? Quand viendra la mort ?

A DAY WITH HER

She looks at me and her eyes are full of blood. And her seductive meat is just cling film wrapping the blood. I can see blood flowing from her sliced breasts. I can see the blood.

She is there. In the morning. And in the evening. I wake up at eight and I think it's the morning. No. It's the evening. It's always the evening.
It's night. Coming back. And it isn't gentle. The night and its puppets of blood with strings running through yellow, translucent flesh. The puppets look like women; the blood flows from the puppets, gently.

The morning. Explosions. Blue everywhere. Always blue; magnificent. The new day, unrelenting. When will life be gentle? When will I be dead?

DIFFÉRENCIATION RUE D'AVRON

Les débris de ta vie s'étalent sur la table :
Un paquet de mouchoirs à moitié entamé,
Un peu de désespoir et le double des clés ;
Je me souviens que tu étais très désirable.

Le dimanche étendait son voile un peu gluant
Sur les boutiques à frites et les bistrots à nègres ;
Pendant quelques minutes, nous marchions, presque
                                                [allègres,
Et puis nous rentrions pour ne plus voir les gens

Et pour nous regarder pendant des heures entières ;
Tu dénudais ton corps devant le lavabo
Ton visage se ridait, mais ton corps restait beau
Tu me disais : « Regarde-moi. Je suis entière,

Mes bras sont attachés à mon torse, et la mort
Ne prendra pas mes yeux comme ceux de mon frère,
Tu m'as fait découvrir le sens de la prière,
Regarde-moi, regarde. Mets tes yeux sur mon corps. »

IDENTITY FORMATION, RUE D'AVRON

The debris of your life spread out on the table:
A packet of Kleenex open and used,
A hint of despair, another set of keys;
I remember you were so very exquisite.

Sunday spread out its glutinous veil
Over the busy chip shops and the Afro bars;
We strolled for a bit with a spring in our step,
And then home again to avoid it all

And to look at each other for hours on end.
You got undressed in front of the sink
Your face had lines but still your body
Was young, you'd say: "Look at me, I'm intact,

My arms are attached to me, and death
Will not still my eyes like my brother's,
You taught me the meaning of prayer,
Look at me, look. Put your eyes on my body."

II

DANS L'AIR LIMPIDE

Certains disent : regardez ce qui se passe en coulisse. Comme c'est beau, toute cette machinerie qui fonctionne ! Toutes ces inhibitions, ces fantasmes, ces désirs réfléchis sur leur propre histoire. Toute cette technologie de l'attirance. Comme c'est beau !
Hélas j'aime passionnément, et depuis toujours, ces moments où plus rien ne fonctionne. Ces états de désarticulation du système global, qui laissent présager un destin plutôt qu'un instant, qui laissent entrevoir une éternité par ailleurs niée. Il passe, le génie de l'espèce.

Il est difficile de fonder une éthique de vie sur des présupposés aussi exceptionnels, je le sais bien. Mais nous sommes là, justement, pour les cas difficiles. Nous sommes maintenant dans la vie comme sur des mesas californiennes, vertigineuses plates-formes séparées par le vide ; le plus proche voisin est à quelques centaines de mètres, mais reste encore visible, dans l'air limpide (et l'impossibilité d'une réunification se lit sur tous les visages). Nous sommes maintenant dans la vie comme des singes à l'opéra, qui grognent et s'agitent en cadence. Tout en haut, une mélodie passe.

IN THE LIMPID AIR

Some say, look at what's happening backstage. How lovely, all that machinery working so smoothly! All these inhibitions and fantasies and desires, all reflected on their own history. The technology of sex appeal. How lovely!
Alas, I'm passionate and always have been about the moments in life when things stop working; when things globally fall apart, like an omen of things to come, not just in the present, but like glimpses of eternity suppressed by the system. The survival instinct on its way out.

I know it's hard to base a code of conduct on such extraordinary suppositions. But that's exactly what we're here for, difficult things. Right now we're suspended in life like on the Californian mesas, those platforms spiralling high over nothing. The nearest neighbour is a few hundred metres away but still in sight in the limpid air (and the impossibility of reunification is written on everyone's face). Right now we're in life like apes at the opera grunting and jumping in harmony. Up above, a melody floats by.

LES ANECDOTES

Les anecdotes, évidemment... Tous les êtres humains se ressemblent. À quoi bon égrener de nouvelles anecdotes ? Caractère inutile du roman. Il n'y a plus de morts édifiantes ; le soleil fait défaut. Nous avons besoin de métaphores inédites ; quelque chose de religieux intégrant l'existence des parkings souterrains. Et bien sûr on s'aperçoit que c'est impossible. Beaucoup de choses, d'ailleurs, sont impossibles. L'individualité est essentiellement un échec. La sensation du moi, une machine à fabriquer le sentiment d'échec. La culpabilité semble offrir une voie intéressante, à condition qu'il fasse beau. Presque impossible à développer. Intelligent et inédit, en tout cas. Grande objectivité.

ON ANECDOTES

Anecdotes, yes of course… All human beings are the same. What's the point of picking off new anecdotes? One of the novel's more futile traits. No more edifying deaths; the sun's gone missing. We need innovative metaphors, something a bit religious, linked up to underground car parks. And then of course that turns out to be impossible. Lots of things aren't possible, in fact. Individuality is essentially a flop. Those feelings of selfhood, nothing but a machine producing a refined sense of failure. Guilt seems an interesting option, provided the weather's nice. Intelligent and innovative, in any case. Objectivity rules OK.

On gémit de souffrance ou de plaisir,
Le cri est également une synthèse.
L'essentiel est finalement de ne pas dormir ;
Parfois on s'étripe, parfois on se baise.

En réalité, je l'ai toujours su, j'étais moins résistant que toi ; les événements récents en administrent une preuve parfaite. Finalement, le plus vulgaire en toi, c'est encore ton rire. C'est le dernier trait qui manquait à l'abjection de ton personnage, pauvre conne.

Naturellement, nous ne savons pas aimer
Comme l'écrivait ta sœur à sa fille
Après son troisième avortement.
C'est quelque chose comme une espèce de secret
Perdu. Pourtant, le soleil brille
Et les évêques perdent leurs dents.

Il est depuis quelques semaines évident pour moi que les expériences n'enrichissent pas l'être humain, mais qu'elles l'amoindrissent ; plus exactement, elles le détruisent. Les gens réfléchissent, ils font la moyenne ; naturellement ça se rapproche de zéro, et même assez vite. Finalement, le plus grand succès de mon parcours terrestre aura été de ne rien pouvoir apprendre, en aucun cas, de la vie.

We moan in suffering or pleasure,
A cry is a synthesis too.
Main thing is not to fall asleep,
Sometimes we hack, sometimes we fuck.

Truth is I've always known I'm less resilient than you, recent events have stuffed that into me. In the end the most vulgar thing about you has always been your laugh. It's the last piece of your vile self, stupid cow.

We don't know how to love each other, of course we don't,
As your sister wrote to her daughter
After her third abortion.
Something like a lost
Secret. But the sun is still shining
And the bishops' teeth are decaying.

For a few weeks now it's been clear to me that experience does not enrich human life, but diminishes it; in fact destroys it. People do their thinking, they average it all out; everything moves to zero and pretty quick at that. At the end of the day the great success of my travels on earth is my inability to learn anything whatsoever about life.

La face de l'homme se détachait avec une éprouvante netteté sur le fond de branchages (humains, nous flairons les humains ; nous les délimitons au milieu d'un espace touffu).

Si nous reconnaissons la Gestalt de l'humain
Dans un environnement franchement défavorable,
Si nous délimitons ses contours de nos mains
Afin que le semblable soit connu du semblable,

Pourquoi la solitude ? Pourquoi l'écrasement ?
Pourquoi dans la poitrine le reptile de l'angoisse ?
Au milieu de la nuit, la langue entre les dents,
Je sens dans mes organes les bactéries qui croissent.

Semblables et différents, nos corps sont envahis par des germes. Différents et semblables, ces germes contiennent le pourrissement, impliquent le désespoir. Ils constituent, cependant, l'essence de la réalité.

The face of man stands out with trying clarity from the tangle in the forest (we humans, we sniff out humans; we see their outline in the undergrowth).

If we can make out the Gestalt of the human
In a frankly unfavourable environment,
If we can shape its lines with our hands
And find the same in the same,

Why loneliness? Why feel crushed?
Why does anxiety slither in the heart?
In the middle of the night, tongue against teeth,
I can feel the bacteria sprout in my guts.

The same and different, our bodies are invaded by germs. Different and the same, the germs shape decay and induce despair. But still they form the essence of lived reality.

Je n'ai jamais pu supporter les trop longs moments d'union avec la nature,
Il y a trop de fouillis et d'animaux qui glissent
J'aime les citadelles qu'on bâtit dans l'azur
Je veux l'éternité, ou au moins ses prémisses.

L'examen attentif du sol d'une pinède fait apparaître une profonde dysharmonie entre ses brindilles. Cette dysharmonie se révèle créatrice d'un monde, et d'un destin pour les insectes. Ils se croisent, chacun préoccupé d'une survie aléatoire. Leur vie sociale paraît limitée.

Je n'ai jamais réussi à accepter les cantates de Jean-Sébastien Bach,
La répartition y est trop parfaite entre le silence et le bruit
J'ai besoin de hurlements, d'un magma corrosif, d'une atmosphère d'attaque
Qui puisse écarteler le silence de la nuit.

Notre génération semble avoir redécouvert le secret d'une musique parfaitement rythmée, et donc parfaitement ennuyeuse. Entre la musique et la vie, il n'y a qu'un pas. Payé par personne, au service de l'humanité, je continue à frotter une par une mes allumettes lyriques. Heureusement, le SIDA veille.

I've never been able to bear lengthy reunions with nature,
Too many tangles and slithering animals
I like citadels in the sky
I want eternity, or at least its principle.

On careful examination the ground in the pine forest reveals a profound disharmony in the twigs. A whole world and the destiny of insects are created in this disharmony. They hurry by tied up in their uncertain future. Their social life seems limited.

I really can't stand the cantatas of J.S. Bach,
The distribution of sounds and silence is too perfect
I need yelling, a corrosive magma, an aggressive approach
Ripping to bits the silence of the night.

In our time we've rediscovered the secret of perfect rhythm, it seems, which means perfectly boring. There's a hair's breadth between music and life. I'm in the pay of nobody, and in the service of humanity, I strike my lyrical matches one at a time. Fortunately, AIDS is watching over us.

Parlons de foin et de fœtus :
Les vaches, parfois, sont nerveuses
Et sous les abris d'autobus
Leur regard douloureux se creuse.

J'admire énormément les vaches
Mais les pouliches, le soir, j'y pense.
J'aurais aimé être un Apache,
Mais je travaille à la Défense.

Si vous connaissez la tour GAN,
Vous connaissez mon existence ;
Regardez la forme de mon crâne,
Imaginez des expériences.

J'aurais aimé une prairie
Immense et grise sous le vent
J'aurais aimé une patrie,
Quelque chose de fort et de grand.

Les pouliches avancent et reculent,
Leur comportement est prudent
Les commerciaux sont des crapules,
Mais ils sourient à pleines dents.

Let's talk of harvest and foetus:
At times the cows look nervous,
Often at bus stops you'll see
Their sad and sunken eyes.

Cows I greatly admire
But fillies at night I wonder.
I wanted to be an Apache
But my job is at la Défense.

If you knew the GAN tower
Then you'd know my life;
See the shape of my skull
Think of days gone by.

I'd have loved a prairie
Vast and grey in the wind
I'd have loved a country
Big and mighty and green.

The fillies move around,
Very shy and demure
Though city gents are rats,
They parade a massive grin.

Quand elle m'apercevait, elle tendait son bassin
Et elle ironisait : « C'est gentil d'être venu… »
J'observais vaguement la courbe de ses seins
Et puis je m'en allais. Mon bureau était nu.

Tous les vendredis soir, je jetais des dossiers
Pour retrouver lundi un bureau identique
Et je l'aimais beaucoup. Elle était pathétique,
C'était une secrétaire à la viande avariée.

Elle vivait vaguement tout près de Cheptainville
Avec un enfant roux, des cassettes vidéo
Elle ne connaissait pas les rumeurs de la ville
Et le samedi soir elle louait des films porno.

Elle tapait du courrier et j'aimais son visage,
Tant elle s'efforçait d'être une obéissante
Elle avait trente-cinq ans ou peut-être cinquante,
Elle allait vers la mort et elle n'avait plus d'âge.

When she saw me she'd sway her hips,
"It's nice of you to visit…" with an ironic smile,
I'd look vaguely at the curve of her breasts
Then leave. My office was bare.

I'd throw out files on a Friday night
Monday the office was still the same
I liked her a lot. She was rather weary,
Her secretary meat had passed its date.

She lived somehow, out by Cheptainville
Her child had red hair, she had a VCR
The hum of the city passed her by
She liked to watch porn on Saturday nights.

She typed up the mail and I liked her face
For she tried so hard to get it right
She was thirty-five or maybe fifty,
With death on the way she was lost in her time.

MIDI

La rue Surcouf s'étend, pluvieuse ;
Au loin, un charcutier-traiteur.
Une Américaine amoureuse
Écrit à l'élu de son cœur.

La vie s'écoule à petits coups ;
Les humains sous leur parapluie
Cherchent une porte de sortie
Entre la panique et l'ennui
(Mégots écrasés dans la boue).

Existence à basse altitude,
Mouvements lents d'un bulldozer ;
J'ai vécu un bref interlude
Dans le café soudain désert.

NOON

Rue Surcouf spreads in the rain,
Its deli in the distance.
An American in love is
Writing her sweetheart.

Little by little life goes by,
Humans with umbrellas
Seek a way out
In panic and ennui
(Fag ends in the mud).

Living at low altitude,
Bulldozers moving about;
I've had a brief interlude
In this abandoned café.

L'INSUPPORTABLE RETOUR
DES MINIJUPES

Dans le métro, les jeunes femmes
Circulent dans une ambiance de drame
Au mois de mai, si désirables ;
Je suis sorti sans mon cartable.

Occasions d'« aventures sexuelles » ?
Jeux savants de la séduction ?
Mes journées sont nettement réelles,
J'accède à la stupéfaction.

L'infini des wagons plombés
Sur la ligne 8 (Balard-Créteil) ;
Le lendemain je suis tombé,
C'était une journée de soleil.

On inaugurait le printemps
À coups de jupettes affolantes,
Je n'avais plus beaucoup de temps
(Et je sentais ma chair vivante).

THE UNBEARABLE COMEBACK
OF MINISKIRTS

Young women in the metro
Wander up and down in the
Tragic attractions of May;
I've left my lunchbox at home.

Chance of a little "affair"?
The knowing moves of seduction?
My days are neat and clear,
Now I'm completeley stunned.

The sealed cars of the Balard-
Créteil slip endlessly by;
Later on I fell on my face
It was a bright and sunny day.

Spring declared open
The seeds of panic
In the flick of a skirt.
My time was running away
(I could feel my flesh alive).

L'Éternité en pension complète,
Découverte individuelle du pays
Soirée disco où les corps s'achètent,
Mais pas d'assurance pour la nuit.

Je suis en système libéral
Comme un loup dans un terrain vague,
Je m'adapte relativement mal
J'essaie de ne pas faire de vagues.

Certains soirs, je nourris l'idée
Que j'ai des amis quelque part
C'est difficile de décider
Que pour la vie, il est trop tard.

Je suis au milieu des vacances
Comme un acteur sans scénario,
Mais je sais que les autres dansent
Et qu'ils se filment en vidéo.

An eternity package, all included,
Personalized local discoveries,
Bodies for sale in the clubs,
But no sex guaranteed for the night.

I stick out in free-market society
Like a wolf on an open plane,
I'm not adapting too brightly
I try to avoid making waves.

Some nights I turn over and over
The idea I have friends out there
It's hard to take in and accept
That for me it's too late to live.

I'm on my summer holiday
Like an actor without a script,
The others are dancing I know
And are making a video.

Les êtres établissent une distance
Qui est prétexte à la franchir ;
Ainsi, dans la soirée, ils dansent ;
Transpiration et repentir.

Je me sens cloué sur ma chaise
Comme un ver blanc trop bien nourri ;
Pourtant les femmes sentent la fraise
Le réséda, le patchouli.

Je me tortille et je me voûte,
J'attends la gifle du destin ;
Comme un chien qui cherche sa croûte,
Je flaire les parfums féminins.

La soirée se prolonge et crève,
Je vais reprendre un Mogadon
Pour aller au pays des rêves :
La nuit, je quitte ma prison.

Humans keep their distance
A reason to get up close,
So they dance the night away
Mixing sweat and repentance.

I'm sat and stuck to my chair
Like a larva too stuffed to morph;
But the women all smell of strawberry
With whiffs of reseda and patchouli.

I wriggle and fidget and hunch
And wait for the crush of fate;
Like a dog looking for lunch,
I delight in the feminine smell.

The evening goes on and goes limp,
More Mogadon later for me
To carry me through to my dreams;
At night I break my own chains.

SÉJOUR-CLUB

Le poète est celui qui se recouvre d'huile
Avant d'avoir usé les masques de survie
Hier après-midi le monde était docile,
Une brise soufflait sur les palmiers ravis

Et j'étais à la fois ailleurs et dans l'espace,
Je connaissais le Sud et les trois directions
Dans le ciel appauvri se dessinaient des traces,
J'imaginais les cadres assis dans leurs avions

Et les poils de leurs jambes, très similaires aux miens
Et leurs valeurs morales, et leurs maîtresses hindoues
Le poète est celui, presque semblable à nous,
Qui frétille de la queue en compagnie des chiens.

J'aurai passé trois ans au bord de la piscine
Sans vraiment distinguer le corps des estivants,
L'agitation des corps traverse ma rétine
Sans éveiller en moi aucun désir vivant.

HOLIDAY CLUB

Poets are lathered in Ambre Solaire
Before the shine of survival runs out
The world was tame in the afternoon
And the palm trees smiled in the breeze

My mind had wandered, I was completely spaced out
I knew the South and the three other ways,
There were vapour trails drawn on the insipid sky
I could see the execs sitting in the planes

And the hairs on their legs, very like mine
And their moral values and their Hindu lovers.
Almost like everyone else, poets
Wag their tails with the other pet dogs.

I'll have spent three years by the pool
Without telling the tourists apart,
The bustle of bodies on my retina
Doesn't prompt any living desire.

La lumière évolue à peu près dans les formes.
Je suis toujours couché au niveau du dallage.
Il faudrait que je meure ou que j'aille à la plage ;
Il est déjà sept heures. Probablement, ils dorment.

Je sais qu'ils seront là si je sors de l'hôtel,
Je sais qu'ils me verront et qu'ils auront des shorts,
J'ai un schéma du cœur. Près de l'artère aorte,
Le sang fait demi-tour ; la journée sera belle.

Tout près des parasols, différents mammifères
Dont certains sont en laisse et font bouger leur queue ;
Sur la photo j'ai l'air d'être un enfant heureux ;
Je voudrais me coucher dans les ombellifères.

Unobjectionably the sun crosses the sky.
I've still got my head on the pavement.
I shall die or go to the beach;
It's seven, I'm sure they're asleep.

I know they'll be there when I leave the hotel,
I know they'll see me, and have on their shorts;
I know the diagram of the heart. By the aorta,
Blood does a U-turn; today will be fine.

Various mammals by the beach umbrellas
Some on a leash and wagging their tails;
In the photo I look like a blissful child;
I'm going to lie in the shade of the weeds.

Nulle ombre ne répond ; les cieux sont bleus et vides,
Et cette mongolienne en tee-shirt « Predator »
Aligne en vain les mots en gargouillis morbides
Pendant que ses parents soulignent ses efforts.

Un retraité des postes enfile son cycliste
Avant de s'évertuer en mouvements gymnastiques
À contenir son ventre. Une jeune fille très triste
Suit la ligne des eaux. Elle tient un as de pique.

Nul bruit à l'horizon, nul cri dans les nuages ;
La journée s'organise en groupes d'habitudes
Et certains retraités ramassent des coquillages ;
Tout respire le plat, le blanc, la finitude.

Un Algérien balaie le plancher du « Dallas »,
Ouvre les baies vitrées. Son regard est pensif.
Sur la plage on retrouve quelques préservatifs ;
Une nouvelle journée monte sur Palavas.

None of the shadows replies;
The sky is blue and empty.
A retard in a "Predator" shirt
Puts her morbid burble in order
And her parents encourage her efforts.

A retired postal worker
Gets into his cycle shorts
And struggles in aerobic routines
To keep his stomach in place.
A very sad young woman
Follows the line of the sea.
She's holding the ace of spades.

No sound in the air, no cry in the clouds;
The day is planned in clusters of habit
The old folk are busy collecting shells;
Today the flat, the blank and the finite.

An Algerian sweeps the floor of The Dallas
And opens the terrace doors. He looks pensive.
On the beach there are condoms lying around;
A brand new day is dawning on Palavas.

SYSTÈME SEXUEL MARTINIQUAIS

On a organisé un papier peint blanchâtre
Pour que les gens y vivent et caressent leurs corps
On n'est pas en vacances pour penser à la mort
En système libéral, parmi tous les mulâtres

Et sous les filaos, les épidermes suent
La journée est très blanche, on se recouvre d'huile
On organise des jeux, le public est docile
Et le soir on déguste des côtelettes de tortue.

Il faut organiser un échange orgastique
Pour que chacun s'amuse et filme en vidéo
Les ébats amoureux, les danses en paréo
Et les fins de soirée un peu paroxystiques.

Ainsi, les êtres humains échangent leurs muqueuses
Avant de tout ranger dans les valises en fibre,
C'est ainsi qu'ils expriment leur statut d'êtres libres
Et leur humanité interchangeable et creuse.

THE MATING RITUALS OF MARTINIQUE

They'd thought eggshell wallpaper would be nice
For people to live by and stroke each other
We haven't gone away to think about death
After all, in a free market, with all the mulattos

Under the filao trees epidermises sweat,
The sun is blinding, we slap on the oil
Games are laid on, the customer's happy
And for dinner we'll try the tortoise chops.

The organizers wanted an orgastic exchange
For everyone to have fun and film it on video
One-night stands, exotic dance
And the night will end in a bit of a trance.

And that's how humans exchange their mucous
Before packing their stuff in their nylon bags,
That's how they express their freedom and their rights
Their standard humanity, hollow and homogenous.

Comme un week-end en autobus,
Comme un cancer à l'utérus,
La succession des événements
Obéit toujours à un plan.

Toutefois, les serviettes humides,
Le long des piscines insipides,
Détruisent la résignation
Le cerveau se met en action.

Il envisage les conséquences
De certaines amours de vacances,
Il aimerait se détacher
De la boîte crânienne tachée.

On peut nettoyer sa cuisine,
Dormir à la Mépronizine,
La nuit n'est jamais assez noire
Pour en finir avec l'histoire.

Weekend on the bus
Cancer in the uterus,
In the sequence of events
There's always a sense.

But towels all humid
Insipid by the pool
Kill off quiescence
And the brain's acceptance.

It fancies outcomes
Of romance and cum
And to leave the fuss
Of a skull concussed.

Keep the kitchen tidy
Get to sleep on tablets
It's never dark enough
To rid ourselves of history.

RÉPARTITION – CONSOMMATION

I. J'entendais des moignons frotter,
    L'amputé du palier traverse
    La concierge avait des alliés
    Qui nettoyaient après l'averse

    Le sang des voisines éventrées,
    Il fallait que cela se passe
    Discussions sur la vérité,
    Mots d'amour qui laissent des traces.

    La voisine a quitté l'immeuble,
    La cuisinière est arrivée
    J'aurais dû m'acheter des meubles,
    Tout aurait pu être évité.

    Puisqu'il fallait que tout arrive,
    Jean a crevé les yeux du chat
    Monades isolées qui dérivent,
    Répartitions et entrechats.

ALLOCATE & CONSUME

I.   I could hear the rub of the stumps,
The amputee opposite was crossing,
The concierge had allies
Washing away the downpour

The blood of disembowelled neighbours,
No way of avoiding it,
Discussions of truth
Words of love and their traces.

My neighbour turned on her heel
The cook was coming in,
Had I bought some furniture
It could all have been avoided.

Since everything had to happen
John dug out the cat's eyes,
Those drifting isolated monads,
Allocation and entrechats.

II.   Au milieu des fours micro-ondes,
      Le destin des consommateurs
      S'établit à chaque seconde ;
      Il n'y a pas de risque d'erreur.

      Sur mon agenda de demain,
      J'avais inscrit : « Liquide vaisselle » ;
      Je suis pourtant un être humain :
      Promotion sur les sacs-poubelle !

      À tout instant ma vie bascule
      Dans l'hypermarché Continent
      Je m'élance et puis je recule,
      Séduit par les conditionnements.

      Le boucher avait des moustaches
      Et un sourire de carnassier,
      Son visage se couvrait de taches…
      Je me suis jeté à ses pieds !

II.   Awash in microwave ovens
      The destiny of every consumer
      Ticks by with every second;
      No chance of an error.

      "Washing up liquid" is written
      Carefully on tomorrow's page;
      I am still a human being:
      Moved by ads on a bin!

      My life changes by the second
      In the Aldi hypermarket,
      I dash forward and back
      Seduced by all the packs.

      The butcher had a moustache
      And a carnivorous smile,
      His face was covered in stains…
      I threw myself at his feet!

III.   J'ai croisé un chat de gouttière,
       Son regard m'a tétanisé ;
       Le chat gisait dans la poussière,
       Des légions d'insectes en sortaient.

       Ton genou de jeune otarie,
       Gainé dans un collant résille,
       Se pliait sans le moindre bruit ;
       Dans la nuit, les absents scintillent.

       J'ai croisé un vieux prolétaire
       Qui cherchait son fils disparu
       Dans la tour GAN, au cimetière
       Des révolutionnaires déçus.

       Tes yeux glissaient entre les tables
       Comme la tourelle d'un char ;
       Tu étais peut-être désirable,
       Mais j'en avais tout à fait marre.

III. I came across an alley cat,
His eyes turned me to stone;
The cat lay in the dust,
Insects in legions coming out.

Your knee like the knee of a young walrus
Was bending ever so quietly
Girdled in a fishnet stocking;
In the night, the absentees twinkle.

I came across an old prole
Looking for the son he'd lost
In GAN Tower, the graveyard
Of disheartened revolutionaries.

Your eyes glided between the tables
Like the turret of a tank;
Very desirable perhaps
But I really couldn't care less.

J'ai marché toute l'après-midi ;
C'était une « activité sportive », en contact avec la nature ;
Pourtant, je suis à nouveau envahi par l'angoisse.

L'hôtel est confortable ;
On ne peut rien lui reprocher, à l'hôtel.
C'est simplement la présence de la vie qui pèse sur moi,
Qui rend les soirées pratiquement impossibles.

C'est la présence ou l'absence de l'esprit qui détermine notre bonheur
Et j'ai eu beau exercer mes muscles toute l'après-midi, aux approches du soir, quelque chose se met à peser sur mon cœur.

Dans la gare de Fontan-Saorge
(Désertée, fermée, carreaux brisés et toilettes bouchées),
Le dernier train de la journée devait passer.

J'ai tiré de mon sac à dos un magazine de rencontres échangistes,
Je l'ai déchiré en deux parts égales
Et j'ai déposé les morceaux près des toilettes « à la turque ».

Les femmes continueront à réclamer des godemichets et de gros sexes blacks
Pour l'improbable plaisir d'un retraité des chemins de fer italiens
Venu visiter la gare où il avait fait sa carrière
Et élevé ses enfants
Avant que l'école ne ferme.

I walked all afternoon;
I was kind of "working out", and getting close to nature,
But still I'm sick with anxiety.

The hotel's comfortable enough,
There's nothing wrong with the hotel,
It's just the presence of life weighing down on me
And making the evenings practically impossible.

It's the presence or absence of hope which determines our happiness:
However hard I exercise my body all afternoon, come the evening, something starts to weigh on my heart.

At Fontan-Saorge station
(Abandoned, closed, windows smashed and toilets blocked)
The last train of the day was on its way, supposedly.

I had a swingers magazine in my backpack,
I tore it in two equal parts
And left the pages by the toilet hole.

The women will go on wanting dildos and big black penises
For the enjoyment presumably of a retired Italian rail worker
Visiting the station where he'd worked all his life
And brought up his children
Before the school was closed.

Les insectes courent entre les pierres,
Prisonniers de leurs métamorphoses
Nous sommes prisonniers aussi
Et certains soirs la vie
Se réduit à un défilé de choses
Dont la présence entière
Définit le cadre de nos déchéances
Leur fixe une limite, un déroulement et un sens ;

Comme ce lave-vaisselle qui a connu ton premier mariage
Et ta séparation,
Comme cet ours en peluche qui a connu tes crises de rage
Et tes abdications.

Les animaux socialisés se définissent par un certain nombre de rapports
Entre lesquels leurs désirs naissent, se développent, deviennent parfois très forts
Et meurent.

Ils meurent parfois d'un seul coup,
Certains soirs
Il y avait certaines habitudes qui constituaient la vie et voilà qu'il n'y a plus rien du tout
Le ciel qui paraissait supportable devient d'un seul coup extrêmement noir
La douleur qui paraissait acceptable devient d'un seul coup lancinante
Il n'y a plus que des objets, des objets au milieu desquels on est soi-même immobilisé dans l'attente,

Insects run about between the stones
In the prison of their morphing
We're prisoners as well
And some nights
Life is just a procession of things
Their whole presence
Shapes and models our decay
Gives it a place, an unfolding and a meaning;

Like the dishwasher which lived through your first marriage
And your separation,
Like the teddy bear which lived through your fits of anger
And when you gave up.

Social animals live in a set number of relations
In which their desires are born, develop, and sometimes become very powerful,
Then die.

Sometimes they die all of a sudden,
Some evenings
There were the habits which make up life and suddenly there is nothing at all
The sky once bearable is suddenly blackened
Pain once tolerable is suddenly piercing
Only the objects are left, like objects we wait, we cannot move,

Chose entre les choses,
Chose plus fragile que les choses
Très pauvre chose
Qui attend toujours l'amour
L'amour, ou la métamorphose.

We're a thing among things,
A thing more fragile than things
A very poor thing
Always waiting for love
For love, or a metamorphosis.

Dans le métro, sur le périf,
La machine commence à tourner
Je m'arrête, soudain attentif :
J'entends la machine exploser

Au ralenti, comme un organe,
Comme un ventricule noirci ;
Au loin j'aperçois la tour GAN,
C'est là que se décide ma vie.

Les cadres montent vers leur calvaire
Dans des ascenseurs de nickel,
Je vois passer les secrétaires
Qui se remettent du rimmel.

Sous les maisons, au fond des rues,
La machine sociale avance
Vers des objectifs inconnus ;
Nous n'avons plus aucune chance.

On the tube, on the ring road
The system is starting up
I've stopped, with a sudden thought:
I can hear it all explode

Slo-mo, like an organ,
A tar-blackened heart;
I can see the GAN Tower
And my life in the balance.

Execs climb to their calvary
In chrome-plated lifts
And secretaries go by
Touching up their mascara.

Under the houses, in the streets' dark corners
Society's machine advances
Towards its invisible goals.
We no longer stand a chance.

Cet homme sur l'autre quai est en bout de course ;
Je ne suis plus tout à fait au début.
Pourquoi est-ce que je ressens de la pitié pour lui ?
Pourquoi, *exactement* ?

Sur le quai, près de moi, il y a des amoureux
Qui ne regardent pas l'homme
(De pseudo-amoureux, car il est déjà chauve).
Cependant, ils s'embrassent ;
Ils semblent croire à l'existence d'un monde entre eux,
D'un autre monde que celui de l'homme,

De l'homme en face
Qui se lève et rassemble ses sacs Prisunic,
Définitivement en bout de course ;
Sait-il que Jésus-Christ est mort pour lui ?

Il se lève, il rassemble ses sacs,
Il clopine jusqu'au bout du quai
Et là, profitant de l'angulation de l'escalier,
Il disparaît.

That man on the other platform has reached the end of his race;
And I am no longer quite at the beginning.
Why do I feel this pity for him?
Why *exactly*?

On the platform, near me, there are lovers
Not looking at the man at all
(Pseudo-lovers, he's bald).
But they're kissing anyway,
They seem to believe there's a world they share,
Another world than that of man,

Or of that man opposite
Who's standing up and gathering his Safeway bags,
Definitely on his last legs;
Does he even know Christ died for him?

He stands up, gathers his bags
Hobbles along to the end of the platform
And there, taking full advantage of that corner of the stairs,
Disappears.

DERNIER REMPART
CONTRE LE LIBÉRALISME

Nous refusons l'idéologie libérale parce qu'elle est incapable de fournir un sens, une voie à la réconciliation de l'individu avec son semblable dans une communauté qu'on pourrait qualifier d'humaine,
Et d'ailleurs le but qu'elle se propose est même tout différent.

Nous refusons l'idéologie libérale au nom de l'encyclique de Léon XIII sur la mission sociale de l'Évangile et dans le même esprit que les prophètes antiques appelaient la ruine et la malédiction sur la tête de Jérusalem,
Et Jérusalem tomba, et pour se relever, elle ne mit pas moins de quatre mille ans.

Il est indiscutable et avéré que tout projet humain se voit de plus en plus évalué en fonction de purs critères économiques,
De critères absolument numériques,
Mémorisables sur fichiers informatiques.
Cela n'est pas acceptable et nous devons lutter pour la mise en tutelle de l'économie et pour sa soumission à certains critères que j'oserai appeler éthiques,

Et quand on licencie trois mille personnes et que j'entends bavasser sur le coût social de l'opération il me prend une envie furieuse d'étrangler une demi-douzaine de conseillers en audit,
Ce qui serait une excellente opération,
Un dégraissage absolument bénéfique,
Une opération pratiquement hygiénique.

A LAST STAND AGAINST
THE FREE MARKET

We reject liberal ideology for failing to show the way, or a route to reconciliation between the individual and his fellow beings
in a community at least to some degree human;
And besides the aim of liberalism is altogether different.

We reject liberal ideology in the name of the social mission of the Gospel
which is enshrined in the papal encyclical of Leon XIII;
We reject liberal ideology in the voice of the Old Testament prophets
calling ruin and destruction down upon Jerusalem.
And Jerusalem fell, and did not rise again for four thousand years.

It is unquestionable and widely accepted that all human endeavour is measured against purely economic criteria
entirely numerical criteria
captured in digital files.
That is not acceptable. We must fight for an economy retrained by the people
and subjected to different standards I would venture to call ethical.

And when three thousand people are laid off and
I hear someone blathering on about the cost in human capital of this adjustment
I am filled with a furious desire to strangle
Half a dozen financial experts,
Which would be an excellent adjustment,
A completely beneficial cutback,
A health-and-safety upgrade.

Faites confiance à l'initiative individuelle, voilà ce qu'ils répètent partout, ce qu'ils vont partout répétant comme ces vieux réveils à ressort dont l'uniforme déclic suffisait généralement à nous plonger dans une insomnie fatigante et définitive,
À cela je ne peux répondre qu'une seule chose, et cette chose ressort d'une expérience à la fois navrante et répétitive,
C'est que l'individu, je veux parler de l'individu humain, est très généralement un petit animal à la fois cruel et misérable,
Et qu'il serait bien vain de lui faire confiance à moins qu'il ne se voie repoussé, enclos et maintenu dans les principes rigoureux d'une morale inattaquable,
Ce qui n'est pas le cas.

Dans une idéologie libérale, s'entend.

Believe in the power of the individual, that's what they all keep saying,
that's what they keep going on about like an old clock with a mechanism loud enough
for relentless and desperate insomnia.
I can only think of one thing to say to that, which is the fruit of a recurring and depressing experience:
the individual, I mean the human individual, is quite honestly a small, cruel and pathetic animal.
And it would be pointless to believe in it at all, unless it were shoved back, fenced in and restrained in the
categorical principles of an unassailable morality.
Which is currently not the case.

In a liberal ideology, I mean.

Le but de la vie, c'est d'aimer
Chacun le dit, chacun le sait
Tes paroles sont inutiles
Je ne sens plus ton corps fragile

Et le but de ma vie s'efface
Droit devant, la tour Montparnasse
Dont les étages au ralenti
S'allument comme un rêve englouti.

Nous traversons le commercial
Comme une enveloppe irisée
Dont les stimuli névrosés
Délimitent un destin brutal.

C'est notre vie, c'est notre mort
Qui se dessinent sur les réseaux
La ville nourrit ses bourreaux
Et le dégoût emplit nos corps.

Expériences inarticulées
J'achète des revues sexuelles
Remplies de fantasmes cruels
Au fond, il faut éjaculer

Et s'endormir comme une viande
Sur un matelas défoncé
Enfant, je marchais dans la lande
Je cueillais des fleurs recourbées
Et je rêvais du monde entier
Enfant, je marchais dans la lande
La lande était douce à mes pieds.

The point of life is to love
Everyone says it, and knows it,
All your words are in vain
Where is your body so frail?

The point of my life escapes me
Tour Montparnasse dead ahead
The levels are slowly rising, and
Come to light like a sunken dream.

As we walk through the shopping centre
In an incandescent coating
Plenty of neurotic stimuli
Define a brutal destiny.

All our life and death
Is burning onto networks,
The city feeds the axe
Our bodies are sick with loathing.

In an unspoken moment of life
I buy an ejaculation
From the pages of a sexual journal
Full of cruel excitation

And collapse like meat
On a clapped-out mattress.
As a child I walked on the moors
I picked the weeping flowers
And dreamt of all the world,
As a child I walked on the moors
And the moors were soft and kind.

Confrontée à l'alternative de l'aurore, Annabelle sentait les ombres de sa jeunesse glisser entre les rideaux. Elle aurait souhaité prononcer un adieu définitif à l'amour. Tout l'y incitait ; le glissement des souvenirs, se disait-elle, aurait dû maintenant lui suffire. Il y avait maintenant la nuit, et les organes malades. Une autre expérience, une autre vie ; moins agréable que la précédente, mais probablement plus brève. Sa voisine avait un caniche ; pourquoi pas elle ? Un caniche ne vous protège pas des voyous ; mais son perpétuel état d'enfance est une joie pour les yeux. Il observe le glissement des rideaux, pousse de légers gémissements en apercevant la lumière du jour. Il reconnaît sa laisse, et son collier. Comme l'homme, il est quelquefois atteint d'un cancer. Il accueille la mort avec courage. Il regarde autour de lui, pousse un bref jappement, et il saute dans la cascade.

Faced with a choice between dawn and dusk, Annabelle watched her youth slipping faintly through the curtains. She would have liked to bid a final farewell to love. Everything pointed to that; the quiet presence of her memories should have been enough to see her through, she thought. Now the night, and sick organs. A new experience, a new life; less pleasant than the one before, but probably shorter. The lady next door had a poodle, why not have one too? A poodle doesn't protect you from thugs; but he's forever playful and that's a delight. He watches the curtains move, and whimpers a bit when the sun comes through. He knows his collar and lead, and like humans sometimes he develops cancer. He meets death with fortitude. He looks around, yelps a bit, and jumps in the water.

Si calme, dans son coma,
Elle avait accepté une certaine prise de risque
(Comme on soutient parfois le soleil, et son disque,
Avant que la douleur devienne trop cruelle),
Supposant que chacun était semblable à elle,
Mais naturellement ce n'était pas le cas.

Elle aurait pu mener une vie douce et pleine
Parmi les animaux et les petits enfants
Mais elle avait choisi la société humaine,
Et elle était si belle à l'âge de dix-neuf ans.

Ses cheveux blonds sur l'oreiller
Formaient une auréole étrange,
Comme un intermédiaire de l'ange
Et du noyé.

Si calme, définitivement belle,
Elle soulevait à peine les draps
En respirant ; mais rêvait-elle ?
Elle semblait heureuse, en tout cas.

She looks so calm, lying in her coma,
She had taken a special risk
(Like looking into the sun, and its orb,
Until the pain gets unbearable)
In thinking they were all the same,
But they were not like her at all.

She could have led a full and quiet
Life with pets and little children
But she'd stayed in human company,
At nineteen she'd been so beautiful.

A strange halo came from
The blond hair on her pillow
Like the land in between
Ophelia drowning and Gabriel.

She looks so calm, and beautiful
And still, her breathing
Hardly lifts the sheets;
Was she dreaming? She seemed
Happy, in any case.

Avant, il y a eu l'amour, ou sa possibilité ;
Il y a eu des anecdotes, des bifurcations et des silences
Il y a eu ton premier séjour
Dans une institution sereine
Où l'on repeint les jours
D'un blanc légèrement crème.

Il y a eu l'oubli, le presque oubli, il y a eu un départ
Une possibilité de départ
Tu t'es couché de plus en plus tard
Et sans dormir
Dans la nuit
Tu as commencé à sentir tes dents frotter
Dans le silence.

Puis tu as songé à prendre des cours de danse
Pour plus tard
Pour une autre vie
Que tu vivrais la nuit,
Surtout la nuit,
Et pas seul.

Mais c'est fini,
Tu es mort
Maintenant, tu es mort
Et tu es vraiment dans la nuit
Car tes yeux sont rongés
Et tu es vraiment dans le silence
Car tu n'as plus d'oreilles
Et tu es vraiment seul
Tu n'as jamais été aussi seul

Before there was love, or the idea of love;
There were anecdotes, and digressions and pauses;
There was the day
Of your first stay
In a serene asylum
Where life was painted cream.

Then we forgot, or we nearly forgot; there was an image of beginning,
The prospect of weighing anchor,
You went to bed late
And lying awake
You knew your teeth would rub
Together quietly
In the night.

Then you thought you'd take dance lessons
For later
For another life
That you'd live at night,
Especially at night,
And never alone.

But it's gone
You died
Now
You really are
In the night
Your eyes gnawed away
You lie very quiet
No ears either

Tu es couché, tu as froid et tu te demandes
Écoutant le corps, en pleine conscience, tu te demandes
Ce qui va venir
Juste après.

You are so alone
Never more alone
You lie there, cold, wondering,
Listening to your body fully alive, you wonder
What's going to happen
Straight after.

III

Sublime abstraction du paysage.

COURTENAY — AUXERRE NORD.

Nous approchons des contreforts du Morvan. L'immobilité, à l'intérieur de l'habitacle, est totale. Béatrice est à mes côtés. « C'est une bonne voiture », me dit-elle.

Les réverbères sont penchés dans une attitude étrange ; on dirait qu'ils prient. Quoi qu'il en soit, ils commencent à émettre une faible lumière jaune orangé. La « raie jaune du sodium », prétend Béatrice.

Déjà, nous sommes en vue d'Avallon.

The sublime gone abstract of the countryside.

JUNCTION 19 COURTENAY-AUXERRE NORD.

We are a few miles from the fortresses of Morvan. Total inertia in the front. Beatrice is by my side. "It's a good car, isn't it?" she says.

The lamp-posts are leaning over in strange poses; they look like they're praying. In any case, they've begun to give off a faint orange-yellow light. "It's the low-pressure sodium," according to Beatrice.

Coming up to Avallon already.

Il faisait beau ; et je marchais le long d'un coteau sec et jaune.
La respiration sèche et irrégulière des plantes, en été... qui semblent prêtes à mourir. Les insectes grésillent, perçant la voûte menaçante et fixe du ciel blanc.

Au bout d'un certain temps, quand on marche sous le soleil, en été, la sensation d'absurdité grandit, s'impose et envahit l'espace, on la retrouve partout. Si même au départ vous aviez une direction (ce qui est hélas fort rare... la plupart du temps, on a affaire à une « simple promenade »), cette image de but s'évanouit, elle semble s'évaporer dans l'air surchauffé qui vous brûle par petites vagues courtes à mesure que vous avancez sous le soleil implacable et fixe, dans la complicité sournoise des herbes sèches, promptes à brûler.

Au moment où une chaleur poisseuse commence à engluer vos neurones, il est trop tard. Il n'est plus temps de secouer d'une crinière impatiente les errements aveugles d'un esprit capturé, et lentement, très lentement, le dégoût aux multiples anneaux se love et affermit sa position, bien au centre du trône, du trône des dominations.

It was nice day; and I was walking along a dry and yellow hillside.
The dry and irregular breathing of plants in the summer... they look like they're dying. The insects buzz, piercing the solid and hostile vault of the white sky.

In the summer when you've walked in the sun for a while a feeling of absurdity takes over, it proliferates everywhere, invades everything, it's just everywhere. Even with a destination in mind (highly rare, sad to say, because most of the time it's just a matter of a "country walk"), that image of a purpose fades, seems to evaporate in the boiling heat cooking you in little bursts as you walk in the unrelenting and unyielding sun, ambushed by the dried weeds about to go up in flames.

It's already too late when a sticky heat starts to tar up your neurones. It's too late for a flick of the mane to shake off the blind confusion of a mind being caught, and slowly, very slowly, the chain of disgust with its legion links coils up and secures its position, right in the middle of the throne, domination of dominations.

Le TGV Atlantique glissait dans la nuit avec une efficacité terrifiante. L'éclairage était discret. Sous les parois de plastique d'un gris moyen, des êtres humains gisaient dans leurs sièges ergonomiques. Leurs visages ne laissaient transparaître aucune émotion. Se tourner vers la fenêtre n'aurait servi à rien : l'opacité des ténèbres était absolue. Certains rideaux, d'ailleurs, étaient tirés ; leur vert acide composait une harmonie un peu triste avec le gris sombre de la moquette. Le silence, presque absolu, n'était troublé que par le nasillement léger des walkmans. Mon voisin immédiat, les yeux clos, se retirait dans une absence concentrée. Seul le jeu lumineux des pictogrammes indiquant les toilettes, la cabine téléphonique et le bar Cerbère trahissait une présence vivante dans la voiture. Soixante êtres humains y étaient rassemblés.

Long et fuselé, d'un gris acier relevé par de discrètes bandes colorées, le TGV Atlantique n° 6557 comportait vingt-trois voitures. Entre mille cinq cents et deux mille êtres humains y avaient pris place. Nous filions à 300 km/h vers l'extrémité du monde occidental. Et j'eus soudain la sensation (nous traversions la nuit dans un silence feutré, rien ne laissait deviner notre prodigieuse vitesse ; les néons dispensaient un éclairage modéré, pâle et funéraire), j'eus soudain la sensation que ce long vaisseau d'acier nous emportait (avec discrétion, avec efficacité, avec douceur) vers le Royaume des Ténèbres, vers la Vallée de l'Ombre de la Mort.

Dix minutes plus tard, nous arrivions à Auray.

The TGV Atlantique glided through the night with terrifying efficiency. The lighting was subdued. Human beings were lying in their ergonomic seats in an environment of off-grey plastic. There was no trace of emotion on their faces. There was nothing to see through the window either, the world was plunged in absolute darkness. Some of the curtains were drawn as well, their acid green matched the dark grey of the carpet rather poorly. The silence was almost complete and was only broken by the hissing Walkmans. Eyes closed, the passenger next to me had withdrawn into an intense absence. The lights coming on and off behind the icons for the toilets, the phone and Cerberus's bar gave an ominous sign of something living in the carriage. Sixty human beings had gathered there.

Long and streamlined, steel grey, with discreet coloured highlights, Atlantic TGV no. 6557 comprised twenty-three carriages. Between fifteen hundred and two thousand people were on it. We were rushing at 300 k.p.h. towards the extreme point of the Western world. I suddenly had a feeling (we were travelling through the night in muffled silence, there was no way of telling our prodigious speed; and the neon lighting provided a pale, slightly funereal luminosity), I suddenly had the feeling that this long steel vessel was taking us (discreetly, efficiently, gently) into the Kingdom of Darkness, into the Valley of the Shadow of Death.

Ten minutes later we arrived at Auray.

Avant, mais bien avant, il y a eu des êtres
Qui se mettaient en rond pour échapper aux loups
Et sentir leur chaleur ; ils devaient disparaître,
Ils ressemblaient à nous.

Nous sommes réunis, nos derniers mots s'éteignent,
La mer a disparu
Une dernière fois quelques amants s'étreignent,
Le paysage est nu.

Au-dessus de nos corps glissent les ondes hertziennes,
Elles font le tour du monde
Nos cœurs sont presque froids, il faut que la mort vienne,
La mort douce et profonde ;
Bientôt les êtres humains s'enfuiront hors du monde.

Alors s'établira le dialogue des machines
Et l'informationnel remplira, triomphant,
Le cadavre vidé de la structure divine ;
Puis il fonctionnera jusqu'à la fin des temps.

A long time ago, way back, there were beings
Who formed a circle to keep the wolves
At bay and stay warm; they were bound to vanish
They were a lot like us.

We're here, our last words are fading,
The sea has gone
For one last time lovers are embracing,
The land is naked.

Above our bodies sound waves rise
and fall and move
around the world,
our hearts are nearly cold
death must surely come, deep and gentle;
Soon, human beings will run off from this world.

The dominion of machines will then be complete
And pure information will triumph and fill
The empty carcass of the absent divine;
And this noise will rule until the end of time.

J'ai revu les cahiers où je notais des choses
Sur les différentielles et la vie des mollusques
D'une écriture hachée ; de longues phrases en prose
Qui n'ont guère plus de sens que des poteries étrusques.

J'ai retrouvé la gare et les lundis gelés
Où j'arrivais trop tard pour le train de sept heures ;
Je marchais sur le quai, m'amusant à souffler
L'air chaud de ma poitrine. J'avais froid, j'avais peur.

Nous arrivons au monde épris de connaissance,
Et tout ce qui existe a le droit d'exister
À nos yeux. Nous pensons que chacun a sa chance.
Mais le samedi soir il faut vivre et lutter
Et déjà nous quittons les abords de l'enfance.

Nous quittons l'innocence du regard objectif,
Chaque chose a son prix qu'il faut déterminer
Les relations humaines entrelacent leurs motifs
Plus nous participons, plus nous sommes captifs ;
Puis la lueur s'éteint. L'enfance est terminée.

As I leafed through the books where I jerkily wrote
My differential calculus and my life of the mollusc,
Lengthy prose with hardly more interest
Than staring through glass at an Etruscan pot,

I remembered the station and the frozen Mondays
When I'd arrive too late for the early train;
I'd pace up and down and blow out the air
I looked at my breath, I was cold, I was scared.

We've arrived at an era taken with knowing
And feel that everything that breathes has a right
To exist. We believe we all get our chance.
But Saturday nights to live is to fight
And for us the land of the child is gone.

We've left innocent objectivity behind
Everything has its price which has to be fixed,
In human relations our motives entwine;
The more participation, the more paralysis.
The glimmer dies out. Playtime is over.

Je ne reviendrai plus jamais entre les herbes
Qui recouvrent à demi la surface de l'étang.
Il est presque midi ; la conscience de l'instant
Enveloppe l'espace d'une lumière superbe.

Ici j'aurai vécu au milieu d'autres hommes
Encerclés comme moi par le réseau du temps.
Shanti sha nalaya. Om mani padme ôm,
La lumière décline inéluctablement.

Le soir se stabilise et l'eau est immobile ;
Esprit d'éternité, viens planer sur l'étang.
Je n'ai plus rien à perdre, je suis seul et pourtant
La fin du jour me blesse d'une blessure subtile.

I will never walk again among the reeds
Which wave in the waters of the tarn.
Nearly twelve; the moment has wrapped
The air in luminous beauty.

Here I'll have lived among other humans
Surrounded like me by the networks of time.
Shanti sha nalaya. Om mani padme hum,
The light is in permanent decline.

Night is settling and the water is still;
Spirit of forever, come here and visit
The stillness of the tarn.
I have nothing left to lose, I am one, but
the dying of the day
wounds me a delicate wound.

MAISON GRISE

Le train s'acheminait dans le monde extérieur,
Je me sentais très seul sur la banquette orange
Il y avait des grillages, des maisons et des fleurs
Et doucement le train écartait l'air étrange.

Au milieu des maisons, il y avait des herbages
Et tout semblait normal à l'exception de moi
Cela fait très longtemps que j'ai perdu la joie
Je vis dans le silence, il glisse en larges plages.

Le ciel est encore clair, déjà la terre est sombre ;
Une fissure en moi s'éveille et s'agrandit
Et ce soir qui descend en Basse-Normandie
A une odeur de fin, de bilan et de nombre.

SEMI-DETACHED LIVING

The train was finding its way in the world,
I was very alone on the old orange seat,
There were wire fences, houses and flowers
And the train was steadily parting the air.

There were pastures between the houses
And everything seemed so perfectly normal
It's a long time since I enjoyed my life
I live in a silence of liquid segments.

The sky is still blue, but the land is dark;
A fracture was forming and growing inside me
This evening light on Lower Normandy
Smells of endings, figures and results.

L'appartenance de mon corps
À un matelas de deux mètres
Et je ris de plus en plus fort,
Il y a différents paramètres.

La joie, un moment, a eu lieu
Il y a eu un instant de trêve
Où j'étais dans le corps de Dieu
Mais depuis, les années sont brèves.

La lampe explose au ralenti
Dans le crépuscule des corps,
Je vois son filament noirci :
Où est la vie ? Où est la mort ?

My body's affinities
With a two-metre mattress;
I keep laughing louder
There are so many parameters.

Once there was joie de vivre
And a moment's respite
In the bosom of Christ,
Then the years were meagre.

The twilight of the living body
In a lamp exploding slowly;
Here's the blackened bulb,
Where is living? Where is dying?

Les antennes de télévision,
Comme des insectes réceptifs,
S'accrochent à la peau des captifs
Les captifs rentrent à la maison.

Si j'avais envie d'être heureux
J'apprendrais les danses de salon
Ou j'achèterais un ballon
Comme ces autistes merveilleux

Qui survivent jusqu'à soixante ans
Entourés de jouets en plastique
Ils éprouvent des joies authentiques,
Ils ne sentent plus passer le temps.

Romantisme de télévision,
Sexe charité et vie sociale
Effet de réel intégral
Et triomphe de la confusion.

TV antennae
Like reception insects
Stick to the skin
Of captive spectators,
Captives on their way home.

If I wanted to be happy
I'd take to the ballroom
Or get a balloon
Like the autistic do

Some live to be sixty
Enchanted by their plastic toys
They experience true joy
Indifferent to time.

TV sentiment,
Sex, issues and donations,
Triumph of the real
And confusion inc.

La respiration des rondelles
Et les papillons carnassiers ;
Dans la nuit, un léger bruit d'ailes ;
La pièce est couverte d'acier.

Je n'oublie pas les gestes secs
De cet adolescent furtif
Qui glissait d'échec en échec
En dépliant son corps craintif.

La respiration des termites
S'accomplit sans aucun effort
Une tension vient de la bite,
S'affaiblit en gagnant le corps.

Quand la présence digestive
Emplit le champ de la conscience
S'installe une autre vie, passive,
Dans la douceur et la décence.

The breath of salami
And of meat-eating moths;
A soft whirr of wings
in the night; the room
is clothed in steel.

I have not forgotten
The gawky movements
Of my stealthy adolescence
Drifting from one failure to the next
Timidly unwinding
The knees and elbows of my body.

The breathing of termites
Seems effortless,
A tension in the dick
Disperses in the body.

When the effects of digestion
Invade the conscious domain
Another life appears, passively,
As if in gentle decency.

En rampant sur le matelas
De notre commune allégeance
Je ne suis plus tout à fait là,
Je ne ressens aucune urgence.

Les gens sont coincés dans leurs peaux,
Ils font danser leurs molécules
Le samedi ils se font beaux,
Puis ils se retrouvent et s'enculent.

Voilà ! Je regarde ma porte,
Elle vient d'une bonne usine
Tout est fini, en quelque sorte,
Je vais coucher dans la cuisine.

Je vais retrouver mes poumons,
Le carrelage sera glacial
Enfant, j'adorais les bonbons
Et maintenant tout m'est égal.

Crawling about on the mattress
We discharge our allegiance;
I'm hardly there,
Urges no longer emerge.

People are confined in their skin,
They push their molecules about
They dress up on Saturday nights
Then meet up and fuck and fight.

And so! I'm looking at my door,
A lovely manufactured thing
We're on the finishing touches now,
I might as well sleep in the kitchen.

I'll go home with my lungs
The tiles will be freezing.
As a child I loved sweets
And now nothing matters.

Dans le train direct pour Dourdan,
Une jeune fille fait des mots fléchés
Je ne peux pas l'en empêcher,
C'est une occupation du temps.

Comme des blocs en plein espace
Les salariés bougent rapidement
Comme des blocs indépendants,
Ils trouent l'air sans laisser de trace.

Puis le train glisse entre les rails,
Dépassant les premières banlieues
Il n'y a plus de temps ni de lieu ;
Les salariés quittent leur travail.

In the train for Dourdan
A girl and her crosswords
I can't make her stop,
It's a sign of the time.

Like blocks in space
Workers move quickly,
They make holes in the air
And leave nothing behind.

The train glides on the rails
Past the start of suburbia
Time and place expelled;
Workers are heading for home.

Dans le métro à peu près vide
Rempli de gens semi-gazeux
Je m'amuse à des jeux stupides,
Mais potentiellement dangereux.

Frappé par l'intuition soudaine
D'une liberté sans conséquence
Je traverse les stations sereines
Sans songer aux correspondances.

Je me réveille à Montparnasse
Tout près d'un sauna naturiste,
Le monde entier reprend sa place ;
Je me sens bizarrement triste.

In the semi-vacant metro
Full of semi-porous people
I imagine silly games
That could've done some damage.

Struck by the sudden impression
Of an inconsequential freedom
I travel serenely through stations
Never thinking of making connections.

I wake up in Montparnasse
Next to a Swedish sauna,
Things fall back into place
And now I feel oddly sad.

Un moment de pure innocence,
L'absurdité des kangourous
Ce soir je n'ai pas eu de chance,
Je suis cerné par les gourous.

Ils voudraient me vendre leur mort
Comme un sédatif dépassé
Ils ont une vision du corps,
Leur corps est souvent ramassé.

Le végétal est déprimant,
À proliférer sans arrêt
Dans la prairie, le ver luisant
Brille une nuit, puis disparaît.

Les multiples sens de la vie
Qu'on imagine pour se calmer
S'agitent un peu, puis c'est fini ;
Le canard a des pieds palmés.

A moment of pure innocence
The absurdity of the kangaroos
Tonight I fell on my face,
I'm surrounded by gurus

Selling me their deadening stuff,
Their old-fashioned valium
And their vision of the body;
Often their bodies are shrunken.

Plant life is depressing
It just spreads everywhere
In the meadow the glow-worm
Shines for a night and then goes.

The endless meanings of life
We dream up to calm us down
Leap about, then are gone,
Ducks have got webbed feet.

Une âme exposée au Soleil,
Tout près de la mer menaçante ;
Les vagues s'écrasent et réveillent
Une douleur sombre et latente.

Que serions-nous sans le Soleil ?
Écœurement, dégoût, souffrance,
Stupidité de l'existence,
Tout disparaît sous le Soleil.

La chaleur de midi exhale
Le corps d'un plaisir immobile ;
Désir de mort, oubli total,
Yeux clos sur un coma tactile.

Sans pitié, la mer se déploie
Comme un animal qui s'éveille ;
Cet univers n'a pas de loi.
Que serions-nous sans le Soleil ?

A soul is exposed to the sun
On the edge of the threatening sea;
As they crash the waves repeat
A dark and ancient wound.

Where would we be without the sun?
Depression, disgust and pain,
The stupidity of living,
It all disappears in the sun.

The heartbeat of the noonday sun
Breathes a moment of pleasure;
A feeling of death, oblivion,
Eyes closed in a sensuous coma.

Without pity, the sea unfurls
Like an animal waking and stretching;
There is no law in this universe.
Where would we be without the sun?

Les corps empilés dans le sable,
Sous la lumière inexorable,
Peu à peu se changent en matière ;
Le soleil fissure les pierres.

Les vagues lentement palpitent
Sous la lumière misérable
Et quelques cormorans habitent
Le ciel de leur cri lamentable.

Les jours de la vie sont pareils
À des limonades éventées
Jours de la vie sous le soleil,
Jours de la vie en plein été.

Bodies piled on the sand
Under the merciless sun
Slowly change into mass;
Heat is cracking the stones.

The waves are slowly beating
In a shabby noonday light,
Cormorants fill the sky
With their usual pitiful cries.

The summer days drift by
Tasting of flat lemonade,
Days of our life in the sun,
Days of our life in July.

L'exercice de la réflexion,
L'habitude de la compassion,
La saveur rancie de la haine
Et les infusions de verveine.

Dans la résidence Arcadie,
Les chaises inutiles et la vie
Qui se brise entre les piliers
Comme une rivière à noyés.

La chair des morts est tuméfiée,
Livide sous le ciel vitrifié
La rivière traverse la ville
Regards éteints, regards hostiles.

The fix on reflexion
And the habit of compassion,
Rancid cups of hate
And the smell of herbal tea.

In Arcadia Villas
Chairs stay vacant
Lives are thrown at the pillars
Like the drowned in Charon's river.

The dead rot
Under the glazed sky
The river runs through the city
Dead eyes, hostile eyes.

La brume entourait la montagne
Et j'étais près du radiateur,
La pluie tombait dans la douceur
(Je sens que la nausée me gagne).

L'orage éclairait, invisible,
Un décor de monde extérieur
Où régnaient la faim et la peur,
J'aurais aimé être impassible.

Des mendiants glissaient sous les gouttes
Comme des insectes affamés
Aux mandibules mal refermées,
Des mendiants recouvraient la route.

Le jour lentement décroissait
Dans un gris-bleu de mauvais rêve,
Il n'y aurait plus jamais de trêve ;
Lentement, le jour s'en allait.

Mist had settled in the mountains
I was sitting by the heater,
Rain was falling gently
(I can feel my stomach churning).

A storm was doing the lights,
Invisibly, for a staging of the world
Where hunger and fear prevailed;
I wish I'd been indifferent.

Poor devils were sliding past
Like insects in a famine;
Mandibles poised, they
Swarmed all over the road.

The day was in decline
In the blue-grey of bad dreams
Nevermore respite,
Slowly the day took its leave.

Je flottais au-dessus du fleuve
Près des carnivores italiens
Dans le matin l'herbe était neuve,
Je me dirigeais vers le bien.

Le sang des petits mammifères
Est nécessaire à l'équilibre,
Leurs ossements et leurs viscères
Sont les conditions d'une vie libre.

On les retrouve sous les herbes,
Il suffit de gratter la peau
La végétation est superbe,
Elle a la puissance du tombeau.

Je flottais parmi les nuages,
Absolument désespéré
Entre le ciel et le carnage,
Entre l'abject et l'éthéré.

I was hovering over the river
Near the carnivorous life of Italy
In the dew the grass was green
I was reaching out for the good.

Killing little mammals
Preserves the balance of nature,
Spilling their guts and bones
Is the basic condition of freedom.

They lie dormant under the grass
You just need to scratch the surface:
Plant life is really marvellous
It's as powerful as the grave.

I was hovering among the clouds
In complete unending despair
Between the sky and endless slaughter,
Between revulsion and the ether.

La peau est un objet limite,
Ce n'est presque pas un objet
Dans la nuit, les cadavres habitent
Dans le corps habite un regret.

Le cœur diffuse un battement
Jusqu'à l'intérieur du visage ;
Sous nos ongles, il y a du sang
Dans nos corps, un mouvement s'engage.

Le sang surchargé de toxines
Circule dans les capillaires
Il transporte la substance divine,
Le sang s'arrête et tout s'éclaire.

Un moment d'absolue conscience
Traverse le corps douloureux
Moment de joie, de pure présence :
Le monde apparaît à nos yeux.

Skin is an object and a limit,
It's barely an object at all
In the night, corpses live
In the body lives regret.

The heart distributes its beats
Into the fibres of the face;
There's blood under our nails
And in our body, motion begins.

Our blood is loaded with toxins
Running through the capillaries,
It conveys the body divine,
Then stops, and darkness is light.

A moment of complete awareness
Passes through the body in pain,
A moment of joy, and pure presence:
The world appears, the world is there.

Il est temps de faire une pause
Avant de recouvrir la lampe.
Dans le jardin, l'agonie rampe ;
La mort est bleue dans la nuit rose.

Le programme était défini
Pour les trois semaines à venir
D'abord, mon corps devait pourrir,
Puis s'écraser sur l'infini.

L'infini est à l'intérieur,
J'imagine les molécules
Et leurs mouvements ridicules
Dans le cadavre appréciateur.

It's time to take a break
And time to cover the lamp,
Death crawls in the garden
Blue in the rose of the night.

The schedule was fixed
For the three weeks ahead,
First my body would rot
Then crash against the infinite.

Infinity is in the fibres,
I can see the molecules
And their ridiculous motion
In an appreciative corpse.

Nous devons développer une attitude de non-résistance
[au monde ;
Le négatif est négatif,
Le positif est positif,
Les choses sont.
Elles apparaissent, elles se transforment,
Et puis elles cessent simplement d'exister ;
Le monde extérieur, en quelque sorte, est donné.

L'être de perception est semblable à une algue,
Une chose répugnante et très molle,
Foncièrement féminine
Et c'est cela que nous devons atteindre
Si nous voulons parler du monde
Simplement, parler du monde.

Nous ne devons pas ressembler à celui qui essaie de
[plier le monde à ses désirs,
À ses croyances
Il nous est cependant permis d'avoir des désirs,
Et même des croyances
En quantité limitée.
Après tout, nous faisons partie du phénomène,
Et, à ce titre, éminemment respectables,
Comme des lézards.

Comme des lézards, nous nous chauffons au soleil du
[phénomène
En attendant la nuit
Mais nous ne nous battrons pas,
Nous ne devons pas nous battre,
Nous sommes dans la position éternelle du vaincu.

What we need now is an attitude of non-resistance to the
[world,
The negative is negative,
The positive is positive,
Things are.
They appear, they are transformed,
Then they simply stop being;
In a way the world is given.

A perceptual being is like seaweed,
Vaguely repugnant and very flabby,
Utterly feminine
And that's what we have to discover
To talk about the world
Simply talk about the world.

We must not follow those who would bend the world to
[their desires,
Their beliefs.
But we can have desires,
And even beliefs
In limited quantities.
After all, we are part of a phenomenal world,
And therefore eminently respectable,
Like lizards.

Like lizards we bask in the light of phenomena,
Waiting for night;
But we will not fight,
We must not fight,
We stay for ever in a position of defeat.

Les hirondelles s'envolent, rasent lentement les flots, et montent en spirale dans la tiédeur de l'atmosphère. Elles ne parlent pas aux humains, car les humains restent accrochés à la Terre.
Les hirondelles ne sont pas libres. Elles sont conditionnées par la répétition de leurs orbes géométriques. Elles modifient légèrement l'angle d'attaque de leurs ailes pour décrire des spirales de plus en plus écartées par rapport au plan de la surface du globe. En résumé, il n'y a aucun enseignement à tirer des hirondelles.

Parfois, nous revenions ensemble en voiture. Sur la plaine immense, le soleil couchant était énorme et rouge. Soudain, un rapide vol d'hirondelles venait zébrer sa surface. Tu frissonnais, alors. Tes mains se crispaient sur le volant gainé de peau. Tant de choses pouvaient, à l'époque, nous séparer.

The swallows take their flight, skimming the waves slowly then rise in a spiral through the lukewarm atmosphere. They do not speak to humans because humans remain fixed upon the Earth.
Swallows are not free. They are conditioned by repeating their orbits geometrically. They slightly modify the angle of attack of their wings and describe spirals that grow further and further away from the established surface of the globe. In short, there is nothing to be learnt from swallows.

Sometimes we would come back together by car. On the vast plain the sunset was massive and red. Suddenly a quick flight of swallows made stripes across its surface. You shuddered then. Your hands were tense on the leather corset of the wheel. At the time, so many things could pull us apart.

IV

NOUVELLE DONNE

à Michel Bulteau

Nous étions arrivés à un moment de notre vie où se faisait sentir l'impérieuse nécessité de négocier une nouvelle donne,
Ou simplement de crever.
Quand nous étions face à face avec nous-mêmes sur la banquette arrière dans le fond du garage il n'y avait plus personne,
On aimait se chercher.

Le sol légèrement huileux où nous glissions une bouteille de bière à la main,
Et ta robe de satin
Mon ange
Nous avons traversé des moments bien étranges

Où les amis disparaissaient un par un et où les plus gentils devenaient les plus durs,
S'installaient dans une espèce de fissure
Entre les longs murs blancs de la dépendance pharmaceutique
Ils devenaient des pantins ironiques,
Pathétiques.

Le lyrisme et la passion nous les avons connus mieux que personne,
beaucoup mieux que personne
Car nous avons creusé jusqu'au fond de nos organes pour essayer de les transformer de l'intérieur

Pour trouver un chemin, écarter les poumons pénétrés jusqu'au cœur

NEW DEAL

For Michel Bulteau

We'd arrived at a point in our lives where we felt the right royal need to negotiate a new deal,
Or just drop dead.
As we sat alone with ourselves on the back seat in the corner of a garage they'd all gone,
We liked to discover each other.

We slipped around on the greasy floor
holding bottles of beer
and your satin dress, my dear,
Those moments were really quite strange.

One by one friends disappeared, the kindest became the hardest,
They settled in the cracks
Between the long white walls of drug dependency
Puppets with an ironic air,
Pathetic.

Lyricism and passion we had our fair share
And much more,
We dug deep into our organs and tried
To transform them from the inside
Looking for a way past the lungs through to the heart
But it didn't work,
Our bodies were so naked.

A procession of death and defeat, and the chosen ones rose to their calvary,
I remember your cousin the morning
He dyed his hair green

Et nous avons perdu,
Nos corps étaient si nus.

Répétition des morts et des abandons et les plus purs montaient vers leur calvaire.
Je me souviens de ton cousin le matin où il s'était teint les cheveux en vert
Avant de sauter dans le fleuve,
Sa vie était si neuve.

Nous n'aimons plus beaucoup maintenant les gens qui viennent critiquer nos rêves,
Nous nous laissons lentement investir par une ambiance de trêve
Nous ne croyons plus beaucoup maintenant aux plaisanteries sur le sens du cosmos,
Nous savons qu'il existe un espace de liberté entre la chair et l'os

Où les répétitions les plaintes
Parviennent atténuées ;
Un espace d'étreintes,
Un corps transfiguré.

And jumped in the river,
His life was never bigger.

We don't like people any more who criticize our dreams,
Slowly we invest in an invasion of respite
We don't buy into jokes about the meaning of the cosmos,
We know there's a space for freedom between flesh and blood

Where repetitions and cries
Are moderated at last
A space for embrace
A body refeatured.

Quand il fait froid,
Ou plutôt quand on a froid,
Quand un centre de froid s'installe avec un mouvement
[mou
Au fond de la poitrine
Et saute lourdement entre les poumons
Comme un gros animal stupide ;

Quand les membres battent faiblement,
De plus en plus faiblement
Avant de s'immobiliser sur le canapé
De manière apparemment définitive ;

Quand les années tournent en clignotant
Dans une atmosphère enfumée
On ne se souvient plus de la rivière parfumée,
La rivière de la première enfance
Je l'appelle, conformément à une ancienne tradition : la rivière d'innocence.

Maintenant que nous vivons dans la lumière,
Maintenant que nous vivons à proximité immédiate de la lumière,
Dans des après-midi inépuisables
Maintenant que la lumière autour de nos corps est devenue palpable,

Nous pouvons dire que nous sommes parvenus à destination
Les étoiles se réunissent chaque nuit pour célébrer nos souffrances et leur transfiguration

When it's cold,
Or rather when you are cold,
When a knot of cold moves dully
Into the pit of your chest
And leaps uncomfortably between your lungs
Like a great stupid animal;

When your limbs flap feebly
More and more feebly
And then flop on the sofa
As though for ever;

When the years pass, flashing lights
In a room full of smoke
You don't remember the scented river,
The childhood river
In keeping with tradition I call it
the river of innocence.

Now that we live in light,
Now that we live in close proximity with light,
In tireless afternoons
Now that the light touching our bodies is in reach,

We can safely say we've come to our destination
The stars gather every night to celebrate our suffering and its transfiguration
Into endlessly mysterious symbols

En des figures indéfiniment mystérieuses
Et cette nuit de notre arrivée ici, entre toutes les nuits,
nous demeure infiniment précieuse.

And this night, the night of our arrival,
amongst all others,
is for us forever precious.

SO LONG

Il y a toujours une ville, des traces de poètes
Qui ont croisé leur destinée entre ses murs
L'eau coule un peu partout, la mémoire murmure
Des noms de villes, des noms de gens, trous dans la tête.

Et c'est toujours la même histoire qui recommence,
Horizons effondrés et salons de massage
Solitude assumée, respect du voisinage,
Il y a pourtant des gens qui existent et qui dansent.

Ce sont des gens d'une autre espèce, d'une autre race,
Nous dansons tout vivants une danse cruelle
Nous avons peu d'amis mais nous avons le ciel,
Et l'infinie sollicitude des espaces ;

Le temps, le temps très vieux qui prépare sa vengeance,
L'incertain bruissement de la vie qui s'écoule
Les sifflements du vent, les gouttes d'eau qui roulent
Et la chambre jaunie où notre mort s'avance.

A LONG FAREWELL TO
THE SOUND OF POETS

There's always a city, and traces of poets
Who have met their destiny within its walls,
Water is leaking, and memory whispers
Names of cities, people, holes in your head.

And it's the same story over and over,
Collapsing horizons and massage parlours
Solitude accepted in the neighbourhood's rules,
Even so people are living and dancing.

They are people of another species, of another race,
Eyes wide alive dancing the dance of cruelty;
We have few friends but we each have the sky,
The infinite kindliness of open spaces;

Time and time so old broods on its return,
The vague murmurs of the passing of life
The howling wind, the water rattling
The yellowing walls of our death approaching.

LA MÉMOIRE DE LA MER

Une lumière bleue s'établit sur la ville,
Il est temps de faire vos jeux ;
La circulation tombe. Tout s'arrête. La ville est si
[tranquille.
Dans un brouillard de plomb, la peur au fond des yeux,
Nous marchons vers la ville,
Nous traversons la ville.

Près des voitures blindées, la troupe des mendiants,
Comme une flaque d'ombre
Glisse en se tortillant au milieu des décombres
Ton frère fait partie des mendiants
Il fait partie des errants
Je n'oublie pas ton frère,
Je n'oublie pas le jeu.

On achète du riz dans des passages couverts,
Encerclés par la haine
La nuit est incertaine,
La nuit est presque rouge
Traversant les années, au fond de moi, elle bouge,
La mémoire de la mer.

THE MEMORY OF THE SEA

A blue light settles on the city,
Time to place your bets;
The traffic is dying down. Everything has stopped. The
[city is calm.
In a leaden fog and with dread in the eye,
We walk into the city,
We drift through the city.

By the bullet-proof cars a group of beggars
Like a splash of darkness
Glides and writhes in the debris,
Your brother is a beggar too
He is a wanderer too
I'm not forgetting your brother,
I never forget how we live.

Buying rice in a covered market,
We're surrounded by hatred
The night is unsafe,
The night is almost red
Over the years, deep in me, moves
The memory of the sea.

UN ÉTÉ À DEUIL-LA-BARRE

Reptation des branchages entre les fleurs solides,
Glissement des nuages et la saveur du vide :
Le bruit du temps remplit nos corps et c'est dimanche
Nous sommes en plein accord, je mets ma veste blanche

Avant de m'effondrer sur un banc de jardin
Où je m'endors, je me retrouve deux heures plus loin.

Une cloche tinte dans l'air serein
Le ciel est chaud, on sert du vin,
Le bruit du temps remplit la vie ;
C'est une fin d'après-midi.

SUMMER IN DEUIL-LA-BARRE

Tendrils creep among the tenacious flowers,
Clouds glide in the scent of emptiness:
Our bodies are filled with the sound of time
It's Sunday. We're agreed on my white jacket

Then I collapse on a park bench
Sleep for a bit, wake up two hours further.

A bell rings in the peaceful air
The sun is hot and there's wine on the table,
Life is filled with the sound of time;
It's late afternoon.

L'aube grandit dans la douceur
Le lait tiédit, petites flammes
Vibrantes et bleues, petites sœurs
Lait gonflé comme un sein de femme

Et le bruit du percolateur
Dans le silence de la ville ;
Vers le Sud, l'écho d'un moteur
Il est cinq heures, tout est tranquille.

Dawn grows gently
Warm milk, little flames
All trembling and blue, little sisters,
Milk swells like a woman's breast

And the coffee percolates
In the silence of the city,
In the South a muffled engine
All quiet, in the morning.

J'ai toujours eu l'impression que nous étions proches, comme deux fruits issus de la même branche. Le jour se lève au moment où je t'écris, le tonnerre gronde doucement ; la journée sera pluvieuse. Je t'imagine te redressant dans ton lit. Cette angoisse que tu ressens, je la ressens également.

La nuit nous abandonne,
La lumière délimite
À nouveau les personnes,
Les personnes toutes petites.

Couché sur la moquette, j'observe avec résignation la montée de la lumière. Je vois des cheveux sur la moquette ; ces cheveux ne sont pas les tiens. Un insecte solitaire escalade les tiges de laine. Ma tête s'abat, se relève ; j'ai envie de fermer vraiment les yeux. Je n'ai pas dormi depuis trois jours ; je n'ai pas travaillé depuis trois mois. Je pense à toi.

I have always felt we were close, like blossoms on a tree. Dawn is breaking as I write you this. There's thunder rumbling somewhere, it'll rain later. I think of you sitting up in bed. The anguish you feel, I feel it too.

We're abandoned by the night
Shaped by the light
People again
Very little people.

Lying resigned on the carpet, I'm looking at the rising light. I can see hair on the carpet, it's not yours. A tiny bug struggles up the fabric. I nod off and wake with a start; I'd really like to close my eyes. I haven't slept in three days; and I haven't worked in three months. I'm thinking of you.

Quand la pluie tombait en rafales
Sur notre petite maison
Nous étions à l'abri du mal,
Blottis auprès de la raison.

La raison est un gros chien tendre
Et c'est l'opposé de la perte
Il n'y a plus rien à comprendre,
L'obéissance nous est offerte.

Donnez-moi la paix, le bonheur,
Libérez mon cœur de la haine
Je ne peux plus vivre dans la peur,
Donnez-moi la mesure humaine.

There was a hard rain falling
On our little house
We were sheltered from danger,
Huddled up to reason.

Reason is like a shaggy dog
Nothing is ever lost
And there is nothing left to learn,
Only the path to obedience.

Give me peace, and happiness,
Free my heart from hatred
I can't go on in fear,
Put me in time with humanity,
Give me the measure of life.

Il existe un pays, plutôt une frontière,
Où la lumière est douce et pratiquement solide
Les êtres humains échangent des fragments de lumière,
Mais ils n'ont pas la moindre appréhension du vide.

La parabole du désir
Remplissait nos mains de silence
Et chacun se sentait mourir,
Nos corps vibraient de ton absence.

Nous avons traversé des frontières de craie
Et le second matin le soleil devint proche
Il y avait dans le ciel quelque chose qui bougeait,
Un battement très doux faisait vibrer les roches.

Les gouttelettes de lumière
Se posaient sur nos corps meurtris
Comme la caresse infinie
D'une divinité – matière.

There is a land, or a last frontier,
Where the light is soft and almost tactile
Humans give each other fragments of light
And have absolutely no sense of the void.

The parable of desire
Filled our hands with silence,
Each one of us felt we were dying,
We were quivering for the want of you.

We had crossed childish borders,
On the second morning
We were close to the sun,
There was something moving in the sky,
A soft beating quivered in the rocks.

Little drops of light
Settled on our painful bodies
Like the eternal caress
Of a god. Matter.

Les couleurs de la déraison,
Comme un fétiche inachevé
Définissent de nouvelles saisons,
L'inexistence remplit l'été.

Le soleil du Bouddha tranquille
Glissait au milieu des nuages
Nous venions de quitter la ville,
Le temps n'était plus à l'orage.

La route glissait dans l'aurore
Et les essuie-glaces vibraient,
J'aurais aimé revoir ton corps
Avant de partir à jamais.

The colours of disbanded reason
Like a small unfinished totem
Give a new shape to the seasons,
Absence fills the summer days.

Buddha's tranquil sun
Slid across the clouds
We'd left the city behind,
And the storm had left the sky.

The road slid in the sunrise
The wipers were vibrating,
I'd have liked to see your body
Again, before leaving for good.

Dehors il y a la nuit
La violence, le carnage
Viens près de moi, sans bruit,
Je distingue une image
Mouvante.

Et les contours se brouillent,
La lumière est tremblante
Mon regard se dépouille
Je suis là, dans l'attente,
Sereine.

Nous avons traversé
Des époques de haine,
Des temps controversés
Sans dimension humaine

Et le monde a pris forme,
Le monde est apparu
Dans sa présence nue,
Le monde.

Outside there is night
Carnage and violence;
Come close, quietly,
I see an image
Stirring.

The light trembles
And the contours blur,
I can see clearly now
I'm waiting, composed,
Serene.

We have come through
Times of hatred,
Periods of unrest
No measure for the human

Then the world took shape
And the world was given
Naked and there,
The world.

LA LONGUE ROUTE DE CLIFDEN

À l'ouest de Clifden, promontoire
Là où le ciel se change en eau
Là où l'eau se change en mémoire
Tout au bord d'un monde nouveau

Le long des collines de Clifden,
Des vertes collines de Clifden,
Je viendrai déposer ma peine.

Pour accepter la mort il faut
Que la mort se change en lumière
Que la lumière se change en eau
Et que l'eau se change en mémoire.

L'Ouest de l'humanité entière
Se trouve sur la route de Clifden
Sur la longue route de Clifden
Où l'homme vient déposer sa peine
Entre les vagues et la lumière.

THE LONG ROAD TO CLIFDEN

West of Clifden, headland,
Where the sky changes to water
Where water changes to memory
At the edge of a new world

Along the hills of Clifden
The green hills of Clifden,
I shall lay down my pain.

For us to live with death
Death must change to light
Light change to water
And water change to memory.

To the west, all of humanity
Gathers on the road to Clifden
On the long road to Clifden
Humans lay down their pain
Between the waves and the light.

Montre-toi, mon ami, mon double
Mon existence est dans tes mains
Je ne suis pas vraiment humain
Je voudrais une existence trouble

Une existence comme un étang, comme une mer
Une existence avec des algues
Et des coraux, et des espoirs, et des mondes amers
Roulés par la pureté des vagues.

L'eau glissera sur mon cadavre
Comme une comète oubliée
Et je retrouverai un havre,
Un endroit sombre et protégé.

Avalanche de fausses raisons
Dans l'univers privé de sens,
Les soirées pleines de privation,
Les murailles de la décadence.

Comme un poisson de mer vidé,
J'ai donné mes organes aux bêtes
Mes intestins écartelés
Sont très loin, déjà, de ma tête.

La chair fourmille d'espérance
Comme un bifteck décomposé,
Il y aura des moments d'errance
Où plus rien ne sera imposé.

Show yourself, my twin, my friend,
Where I go is in your hands
I'm still not really human
I'd like a life unfocused

And to exist like a pond, like the sea,
Among the algae
And the coral, and the hopes, and the bitter worlds
Shaped by the clarity of the swell.

The water will slide over my corpse
Like an extinct and forgotten comet
I'll find another refuge
Shady and protected again.

A flood of rationalization
A universe without direction,
Evenings full of want
Under the great walls of decay.

I'm like a gutted mackerel
My organs have been fed to the pigs
My scattered intestines
Are already far, so far, from my head.

Flesh teems with hope
Like a rotting burger,
In the future there will be moments to wander
When commandments and imperatives have vanished.

Je suis libre comme un camion
Qui traverse sans conducteur
Les territoires de la terreur,
Je suis libre comme la passion.

I'm as free as a truck
Without a driver crossing
The valleys of terror,
I'm as free as passion.

POÈME À MARIE-PIERRE

La clarté paraît dangereuse
Et les femmes ont rarement besoin
D'être satisfaites de leur sexe,
Évidemment.

L'avantage d'avoir des organes sexuels internes,
Je le lis avec clarté dans ton regard
Au demeurant presque innocent.
Tu attends ou tu provoques,
Mais au fond tu attends toujours
Une espèce d'hommage
Qui pourra t'être donné ou refusé.
Et ta seule possibilité en dernière analyse est d'attendre.
Pour cela, je t'admire énormément.

En même temps tu es si faible et si soumise,
Tu sais qu'une quantité excessive de sueur diminuera le
[désir
Que je suis seul à pouvoir te donner
Car tu n'en veux pas d'autre,
Et tu as besoin de ce désir.
Pour cela, aussi, je t'admire énormément.

En même temps tu as cette force terrifiante
De ceux qui ont le pouvoir de dire oui ou de dire non
Cette force t'a été donnée
Beaucoup peuvent te chercher, certains peuvent te trouver
Ton regard est la clef de différentes possibilités d'existence
et de différentes structurations du monde
Tu es la clef offerte par la vie pour un certain nombre
d'ailleurs

A POEM FOR MARIE-PIERRE

Having the light on is dangerous
But women rarely worry about
How their organs look,
Obviously.

I can see clearly in your eyes
The advantage of having sex organs inside
It's quite innocent in fact.
You're waiting or being inviting
But either way you're waiting
For a kind of reverence
Which may be shown you, or not,
And in the end your only option is to wait.
And I love you for that.

At the same time you are so weak and submissive
You know an excessive amount of sweat will reduce the need
Which you only feel with me
Because you want no other
And you need me to want you.
And I admire you so much for that.

At the same time you have the terrifying power
To say yes or say no
It is given you
Many may look for you, few will find you
Your look is the key to new combinations, new ways for us to fashion the world
You are the key to life and not just for me,
To many places,
Just touching you I am a better man, all the time,
And I admire you too, for your strength.

À ton contact, je deviens progressivement meilleur
Et j'admire, également, ta force.

Je suis en présence de toi
Comme devant un autre monde
Pourtant, je vais au fond de toi
Je m'arrête, j'écoute les secondes

Et il y a un autre monde.

In the presence of you
I face another world
But I'm going deep inside you,
I keep still, I hear the seconds.

And there is another world.

NAISSANCE AQUATIQUE D'UN HOMME

Il y a d'abord cet acte qu'il faut bien qualifier de charnel,
Faute d'un meilleur terme
Acte où nous engageons pourtant une bonne partie de nos ressources spirituelles
Et de nos croyances
Car nous créons les conditions, non seulement pour un être, mais aussi pour le monde, d'une nouvelle naissance,
Nous en fixons l'initiation et peut-être le terme.

Il y a ensuite cette espèce d'être animal
Qu'on a bien du mal à mettre en rapport avec la femme
Telle que nous la connaissons
Je veux dire, la femme de nos jours,
Celle qui prend le métro
Et qui n'est plus capable d'amour.

Il y a ce geste de l'embrassement qui remonte si naturellement vers les lèvres et vers les mains
Devant l'objet fripé qui sort
Qui était protégé il y a quelques instants encore
Qui vient brutalement de tomber en direction de l'humain
De manière irrémédiable
Et nous pleurons, nous aussi, cette chute.

Il y a cette espèce de croyance en un monde délivré du mal
Et des cris, et de la souffrance,
Un monde où envisager l'horreur de la naissance
Comme un acte amical

Je veux dire, un monde où l'on pourrait vivre
Depuis le premier instant

LIQUID BIRTH

First there is the act we'll just have to call carnal,
For lack of a better word,
Though we invest a lot of our spiritual energy
and our beliefs as well;
We create the conditions not only for the life of one being
but the world, and for a new birth,
We determine the beginning and maybe the end.

Then there is that animal being
Hard for us to relate to a woman
as we would know her
I mean the modern women we know
who takes the metro
no longer able to love.

Then we take it in our arms
it comes so naturally up to our lips
and into our hands;
The crushed thing
so protected a few seconds ago
has brutally dropped into the human
irreversibly
We weep as well for this fall.

There is that belief in a world free of wrong
And cries, and suffering,
A world where the horror of birth is
embraced like a friend.

I mean, a world where we could live
right from the first moment

Et jusqu'à la fin, jusqu'au terme naturel ;
Un tel monde n'est en aucun cas décrit dans nos livres.

Il existe, potentiel.

until the last, until the natural end;
Such a world has never been written about in our books.

It's there, at least possible.

C'est comme une veine qui court sous la peau, et que l'aiguille cherche à atteindre,
C'est comme un incendie si beau qu'on n'a pas envie de l'éteindre,
La peau est endurcie, par endroits presque bleue, et pourtant c'est un bain de fraîcheur au moment où pénètre l'aiguille
Nous marchons dans la nuit et nos mains tremblent un peu, pourtant nos doigts se cherchent et pourtant nos yeux brillent.

C'est le matin dans la cuisine et les choses sont à leur place habituelle,
Par la fenêtre on voit les ruines et dans l'évier traîne une vague vaisselle,
Cependant tout est différent, la nouveauté de la situation est proprement incommensurable,
Hier en milieu de soirée tu le sais nous avons basculé dans le domaine de l'inéluctable.

Au moment où tes doigts tendres petits bêtes ont accroché les miens et ont commencé à les presser doucement
J'ai su qu'il importait très peu que je sois à tel moment ou à tel autre ton amant
J'ai vu quelque chose se former, qui ne pouvait être compris dans les catégories ordinaires,
Après certaines révolutions biologiques il y a vraiment de nouveaux cieux, il y a vraiment une nouvelle Terre.

It's like a vein under the skin being chased by a needle
It's like a beautiful fire no one wants to put out,
The skin has got tough, even blue in places, but
still the body is refreshed as the needle pierces
We're walking in the dark, our hands tremble a bit, still
our fingers touch lightly and our eyes are shining.

Morning in the kitchen and everything in its place,
There are ruins through the window and a couple of dishes in the sink,
But everything is different, the novelty of the thing
is properly incommensurable,
Yesterday evening you know we suddenly fell into
the unavoidable.

Just when your fingers the tender little beasts
hooked up with mine and began gently to squeeze
I saw it didn't matter when I'd be your lover and when again
I saw something take shape, we'll never understand it with
the categories we have,
In the paradigm shifts of biology another sky really
appears, there really is a new Earth.

Almost nothing happened, we're unsteady from the high
Something has started to move, like opium or Christ,
forces that don't make any deals; the victims of love
begin as willing victims
And the life circulating in our veins this morning
has intensified to a prodigious extent.

Il ne s'est à peu près rien passé et pourtant il nous est impossible de nous délivrer du vertige,
Quelque chose s'est mis en mouvement, des puissances avec lesquelles il n'est pas question qu'on transige,
Comme celles de l'opium ou du Christ, les victimes de l'amour sont d'abord des victimes bienheureuses
Et la vie qui circule en nous ce matin vient d'être augmentée dans des proportions prodigieuses.

C'est pourtant la même lumière, dans le matin, qui s'installe et qui augmente,
Mais le monde perçu à deux a une signification entièrement différente
Je ne sais plus vraiment si nous sommes dans l'amour ou dans l'action révolutionnaire
Après que nous en avons parlé tous les deux, tu as acheté une biographie de Maximilien Robespierre.

Je sais que la résignation vient de partir avec la facilité d'une peau morte,
Je sais que son départ me remplit d'une joie incroyablement forte,
Je sais que vient de s'ouvrir un pan d'histoire absolument inédit
Aujourd'hui et pour un temps indéterminé nous pénétrons dans un autre monde, et je sais que dans cet autre monde tout pourra être reconstruit.

The light is the same in the morning, settling, intensifying,
But the world sensed together has a meaning
quite different
I'm not sure if this is love or revolution
We talked and later you bought a biography of Robespierre.

Giving up has flaked away like dead skin
And I know the space left behind
is filled with unbeatable joy,
A new way of history has appeared
never seen before,
Today and indefinitely we're walking into another world
and I know
in the other world we can rebuild everything.

LE SENS DU COMBAT

Il y a eu des nuits où nous avions perdu jusqu'au sens
[du combat
Nous frissonnions de peur, seuls dans la plaine
[immense,
Nous avions mal aux bras
Il y a eu des nuits incertaines et très denses.

Comme un oiseau blessé tournoie dans l'atmosphère
Avant de s'écraser sur le sol du chemin
Tu titubais, disant des mots élémentaires,
Avant de t'effondrer sur le sol de poussière ;
Je te prenais la main.

Nous devions décider d'un autre angle d'attaque,
Décrocher vers le Bien
Je me souviens de nos pistolets tchécoslovaques,
Achetés pour presque rien.

Libres et conditionnés par nos douleurs anciennes
Nous traversions la plaine
Et les mottes gercées résonnaient sous nos pieds ;
Avant la guerre, ami, il y poussait du blé.

Comme une croix plantée dans un sol desséché
J'ai tenu bon, mon frère ;
Comme une croix de fer aux deux bras écartés.
Aujourd'hui, je reviens dans la maison du Père.

THE WAY OF THE STRUGGLE

There were nights when we lost even our sense of the
                                              [struggle
We shuddered with fear, alone in the colossal plain,
Our arms were hurting
There were very dense and uncertain nights.

Like an injured bird circling in the air
Before crashing on the hard ground of our way
You were staggering, saying elemental words,
And collapsing on the dusty way;
I took your hand.

We had to find another angle of attack
Take off towards Good
I remember our Czech guns
Worth only a coin or two.

Free and conditioned by our ancient sufferings
We walked across the plain
The frozen clods echoed under our feet;
Before the war, friend, in this soil grew wheat.

Like a cross stuck in dry ground
I held on, brother
Like an iron cross, with my arms spread wide.
Today, I come back to the house of the Father.

DELPHINE GRASS has written a doctoral thesis entitled *The Poetics of Humanity in the Novels of Michel Houellebecq* at University College London. Her poetry has been published in various French and English-language journals. She is a member of the A Verse poetry group based in La Sorbonne, Paris.

TIMOTHY MATHEWS is Professor of French and Comparative Criticism at University College London. He is author of *Reading Apollinaire. Theories of Poetic Language* (Manchester University Press 1987 and 1990), and *Literature, Art and the Pursuit of Decay in Twentieth-Century France* (Cambridge University Press 2000 and 2006). He is currently preparing a book entitled *Where is Alberto Giacometti?* He is co-editor with Jan Parker of *Tradition, Translation, Trauma: the Classic and the Modern* (OUP, 2011). He wrote the Introduction to *One Poem in Search of a Translator* edited Eugenia Loffredo and Manuela Perteghella (Peter Lang 2009). With Luce Irigaray he translated her *Prières quotidiennes / Everyday Prayers* (Maisonneuve & Larose and University of Nottingham Press, 2004), and he is translating Gérard Macé, *Illusions sur Mesure/Illusions Made to Measure* (Gallimard, 2004).